WHY AREN'T YOU OVER THIS BY NOW?

How Trauma Messes You Up and What to Do About It

T. Susan Bachmann, MEd, LPC, RPT, NCC,
EMDR Certified Therapist,
Amen Clinic Certified Brain Health Coach

Kelly A. James, PhD, LPC, RPT-S, NCC, CCTP,
CATP, CPC, Emotion Code Certified,
EMDR-Trained

Why Aren't You Over This By Now © 2018 by Susan Bachmann and Kelly James. All Rights Reserved.

All rights reserved. No part of this book may be reproduced in any form or by any electronic or mechanical means including information storage and retrieval systems, without permission in writing from the authors. The only exception is by a reviewer, who may quote short excerpts in a review.

Cover Artwork By Kelly James

Susan Bachmann
Visit my website at www.ftrctulsa.org
Kelly James
Visit my website at www.drkellyajames.com

Printed in the United States of America

First Printing: October 2018

ISBN-97 817-9-0397778

Contents

1: This is Why You Are Not Over This By Now 6
2: This is Trauma 12
3: It's Not Really in the Past 19
4: Beliefs Are the Core 24
5: Parts of You 34
6: The Monsters in the Bottom Drawer 39
7: How Did Your Brain Get This Way 47
8: Trauma Glasses 57
9: Magnet Moments 62
10: How to Know 68
11: Who to Choose 73
12: Recap! 77
Appendix 79
Image A 93
About the Authors 94
Endnotes 97

Acknowledgments

We would like to acknowledge Dean Williams and Janice Ross, of Green Country Behavioral Health, Muskogee, OK for introducing us to the work of Dr. Bruce Perry and Dr. Rick Gaskill at the beginning of our professional careers. Their work guided our professional development as child therapists with an emphasis on neurobiology. We want to express gratitude for the work of Dr. Bessel van der Kolk that has contributed significantly to our continued professional development.

A client planted the seed for this book several years ago. I owe her gratitude and appreciate the honor it was to help her walk her path of healing. All of the people who have allowed me to walk with them and help them move toward a place of wholeness have not only taught me much about how fragile children are, how courageous they are and how resilient they are, they have given me a great honor by allowing me to be part of their lives. Thank you.

T. Susan Bachmann

To T. Susan Bachmann – thank you for asking me to co-author this project with you. Even though we spent many hours together writing and rewriting, we were single focused on the goal of helping individuals know how their life experiences have impacted them and that getting therapeutic help will change their life, forever.

I would like to express my sincere gratitude to the clients who have taught me so much about the experiences of trauma and the durability of the human spirit to survive genuinely horrific events. Their desire to live a life free of the pain of the past encouraged me to learn more about the therapeutic approaches that would help them most. I have been privileged to walk with these clients to witness their courage, strength, and determination, on their path to emotional wellness.

Kelly A. James

We would like to extend our appreciation and gratitude to our research assistant, Megan Buker Murray. She was invaluable in helping us get this book ready for publication.

We extend great appreciation to Austin Stember for his time in helping get this book published.

PREFACE STATEMENT

The information in this book is intended to help individuals who have suffered from any distressing event or trauma to increase his or her understanding of the impact of trauma and encourage them to seek treatment.

We wrote this book for those individuals who are *not* familiar with how the brain processes trauma.

This book is not intended to provide new or in-depth information for those working in the field of trauma therapy.

Message:
The names and details of the individuals in the case studies have been altered to protect their privacy.

1

THIS IS WHY YOU ARE NOT OVER THIS BY NOW

"Traumatized people chronically feel unsafe inside their bodies. They learn to hide from their selves"
                                    −BESSEL VAN DER KOLK

I was a nine-year-old little girl who liked to play with Barbie dolls, ride bikes, play softball, and play with my fluffy white poodle. When the abuse started, I did not know anything about anything, much less about sex. After it started, I only knew I felt shamed, guilty, alone, damaged, and responsible. I was told it was my fault, and I believed him. He stole my innocence, and it felt like he stole my life. My introduction to sex was hostile, horrible, and shameful. Not only did I feel like damaged property; I *believed* I was damaged property, so I kept silent. I did not tell anyone, not a single person until my 20's. I remained paralyzed in silence until my 30's. I was in survival mode and scared, all the time, but had to pretend that I was fine. Remaining silent, however, was costly. I could not trust anyone and felt like an agitated volcano all the time. I often wondered how different my life would have been had I been able to tell someone, so that the abuse could have stopped. I wondered how different my life would have been if I had had counseling to heal the wounds of abuse when I was a child.

I did not get counseling as a child. It wasn't until my 30's that I started going to therapists. I benefited from the therapy, but it did not decrease my level of anger. When we moved, I would find another therapist. It seemed to help, but then I would get triggered, and all that rage would come boiling out. It would take me weeks to figure out what caused that degree of anger and rage. I kept searching for answers. I kept trying to heal myself because I did not like the way I felt, but the volcano was still there. I had gotten very good at hiding the volcano. Most people would have been surprised to know I was that angry, but it was always churning, ready to erupt at any moment. Then I found a therapy that healed the emotional memories stored in the state-level drawer (more on the state-level drawer later!) I worked diligently to heal those childhood memories because I wanted to feel better; I wanted to feel something other than a volcano. After the healing work, the volcano disappeared. I feel peaceful all the time now; I feel emotionally whole and emotionally balanced. It is not true that children are resilient or that they are too young to remember. Children are vulnerable and fragile, and can suffer in silence for many years, as I did.

This book is intended to help you understand how trauma may have affected you, understand the process

of trauma therapy with actual case examples, help you decide when to seek professional help and to introduce you to the different options for therapy

We are therapists who started our careers working with children in foster care and with the parents of those children. All those children had experienced abuse or neglect and as a result were separated from their biological families. Many of the parents had experienced childhood abuse, so repeating the pattern of abuse was natural for them. Some of those parents were addicted to drugs and alcohol; as a result, they neglected their children. Friends used to comment that they could not do what we did. For our friends, the thought of someone hurting children was too much, and something they did not want to think about, much less hear about. We knew those children needed someone who would listen to their stories and allow them to express their fear, sadness, betrayal, and pain without being criticized or judged. They lived in homes where the adults told them their negative behaviors were the reason the family was experiencing difficulties, that they were not good enough, and that something was wrong with them. By the time we started working with these children, many already had a core belief that they were terrible and no good. All those children had experienced some type of trauma.

Our friends would not have wanted to hear about what happened to those children. They also did not want to imagine what happened to those children as they grew into adults. The aftermath of trauma can include, but is not limited to, lasting anger, anxiety, depression, fear, sadness, nightmares, broken relationships, failing grades in school, lost jobs, alcohol and substance abuse and physical illnesses. Like the friends and family members who don't want to think about the bad things that happened, the people it happened to don't want to think about it either. All too often they grow up with a sense that they should be able to handle it and get over it without help, but maybe they can't. We would venture to say that it is the unusual person who can get past their past without some assistance.

When Susan moved away from working with abused children to start working with adults in an outpatient behavioral health setting, her supervisor insisted she worked with the "worried well." Typically, the "worried well" are successful, well-functioning people with a bit of difficulty such as getting through a transition, choosing a career, or raising children. Susan often argued that there were no "worried well" among her clients. Kelly worked as an Employee Assistance Program therapist for a time. The clients she saw were also supposed to be the "worried well," but one of her client's children had been murdered a month before she came to therapy, another client's baby died, and another child client's mother had been diagnosed with stage four cancer and given two months to live. There is nothing *worried well* about any of those issues.

"It is the rare child who escapes trauma entirely"
-Dr. Bruce Perry

Research of 18,000 middle-class people from Orange County California in the 1990s, known as the ACEs (Adverse Childhood Experiences) study[1], reported physical abuse in 28% of the participants and sexual abuse in 21%. This statistic shows that almost one-third of people have experienced physical abuse and one in four people has suffered sexual abuse. The ACEs study further reported that 40% of the group had experienced two or more of a list of significantly bad experiences. The list included physical abuse, sexual abuse, emotional abuse, physical neglect, emotional neglect, one's mother treated violently, substance abuse in the family, mental illness in the family, parental separation or divorce, or an incarcerated family member. Eight out of a group of 20 people will have had two or more of those bad experiences. The population of the United States is over 300 million; 40 percent of the American population would be over 120 million people. You may be one of those 120 million individuals, or you know someone who is among that number. Dr. Bruce Perry, Senior Fellow of the Child Trauma Academy in Houston, Texas, and an internationally recognized expert on the impact of early trauma on development said, "It is the rare child who escapes trauma entirely." [2]

Trauma does not discriminate. Trauma is widespread among all cultures, races, and genders. Oftentimes, family and friends tell a person they should just get over the traumatic event. Many people believe they should be able to cope with the trauma, get past it, just get over it, or read a book since there is a wealth of trauma self-help books available. A recent Google search for trauma self-help books resulted in over 1,300,000 matches.[3] So, why are there so many self-help books? Why do people still feel the same way after purchasing the books? Many of our clients report that they felt little or no relief after reading self-help books. One possible reason they do not work could be that people purchase books and never read them. Another reason could be that after reading the book, they do not know how to implement the suggestions. Or, the reason could be that memories of past events are stored in the subconscious mind, whereas the conscious mind reads the self-help book, and people need therapeutic assistance in getting past their past.

This book is intended to help you understand how trauma may have affected you, understand the process of trauma therapy with actual case examples, help you decide when to seek professional help, and to introduce you to the different options for therapy.

This book includes a definition of trauma, a brief introduction to brain development, how trauma can affect the development of core beliefs, and how core beliefs influenced by trauma can cause difficulties in life, what occurs when trauma happens during childhood, and how trauma has shaped who you are now. The words *distressing events* and *trauma* will be used interchangeably throughout the book. Distressing events can be anything that causes anxiety, sorrow, fear, or pain. According to Dr. Bruce Perry, trauma is "not just the past experience but the imprint left on the mind, brain, and body that has on-going consequences."[4] Without therapeutic intervention, the imprint, or the way a person perceives a traumatic event, can negatively impact him for the rest of his life. Therapy can help heal the wounds that are left by traumatic events, so you can live the life you choose rather than a life dictated by past experiences.

Therapy cannot make you who you were before the trauma happened. What therapy can do is help you accept what happened, heal, and integrate the memories into your new life story. Integration means combining the memories, thoughts, and feelings about what happened so that the experience becomes just another *part* of your story, not your whole story. When you can remember and talk about memories without feeling upset, distressed, guilty, or ashamed, then you know the memories are healed and integrated. Healing traumatic memories is the goal of trauma therapy and is possible with help from a trained mental health professional.

Names changed throughout the book

2

THIS IS TRAUMA

"After all, when a stone is dropped into a pond, the water continues quivering even after the stone has sunk to the bottom"
—ARTHUR GOLDEN

On a bitterly cold winter day, Linda* looked out of her window to see two children, who seemed to be about four and five years old, outside in her yard wearing only diapers. Linda walked outside and the children told her they were looking for food. Linda took them into her home, wrapped them in blankets, fed them, and called the police. When the police went to the children's home, they found no adults. What they did find was knee-deep trash throughout the living room and kitchen, bugs, mice, and only rotting food. One police officer said he felt chills and the hair stood up on the back of his neck when he saw the door to the children's room locked with a hasp lock from the outside. Inside that bedroom were a few blankets on the floor, no access to a bathroom, food, or warm clothes. The two children, Miles and Evie,* who were three and four years old, had managed to get out a window to look for food. When Child Protective Services came to the home, they removed 50 large bags of trash from the house. Miles and Evie were placed in foster care and later adopted. They never went back to that house or to the parents who severely neglected them. When their adoptive mother brought them to therapy, Miles hid under a table at the sight of me holding, rocking, and singing to a baby doll. Seeing someone nurturing a baby was so strange to him that he hid.

*Names changed for protection of individuals involved

Miles and Evie's experience was undoubtedly traumatic. Their discovery could have been traumatic for Linda, the police officers, and the child protective services workers. These individuals took in the children, then saw the filth, the lock on the door, the open window, and imagined what it felt like for those children to be hungry, cold, and locked in a stark room. Whether Linda, the police officers, or the child protective services workers experienced what they saw as traumatic depends. It depends on their histories, beliefs, their point of view, and whether they processed the experience without becoming numb or jaded. Every person perceives events differently based on his or her personality and life experiences, including all early childhood and family experiences. What makes occurrences traumatic is the physical and emotional reaction of the people who experience them. The following Big T traumas are examples of events that are almost always traumatic.

Traumatic Events

Big T Traumas

War, Combat, Abuse, Neglect, Car Accidents, Prolonged or Painful Medical Treatment, Torture, Kidnapping, Natural Disasters – Hurricanes, Tornadoes, Earthquakes, Fires

Small t Traumas

Being laughed at, Being made fun of, Doing poorly in school, Being picked on, Moving from one house to another, Losing a cherished belonging

The above are examples of small t events that can be perceived as traumatic depending on a person's personality and life experiences.

The Cambridge Dictionary defines trauma as "severe emotional shock and pain caused by an extremely upsetting experience."[5] But, defining trauma doesn't end there. The definition of a traumatic event, as a requirement for the diagnosis of Post-Traumatic Stress Disorder (PTSD), according to the Diagnostic and Statistical Manual V (DSM V),[6] says that the event must include 1) the occurrence or risk of physical injury or death, to yourself or someone else, 2) the experience of feeling helpless or out of control and 3) the experience of feeling horrified or terrified.

PTSD means you get hurt, think you are going to get hurt, think you are going to die or see something horrible happen to someone else. It also means that during the event you feel helpless and out of control (because you are). The event is endured, but cannot be changed, stopped, or avoided. Horror and terror mean feeling extremely afraid or feeling repulsed, revolted, disgusted, or "grossed out." Traumatic events overwhelm, or unbalance, our usual ability to cope with unpleasant experiences. Researchers Howard and Crandall state that as many as 50% of people will experience a traumatic event, but not all those individuals will develop a Post-Traumatic Stress Disorder diagnosis.[7]

Experiences that may not be as frightening or dangerous as the above can still be hard to get over. Presented in the appendix is Eye Movement Desensitization Reprocessing Therapy (EMDR), an effective therapy for healing traumatic memories. EMDR literature refers to "big T", (as in capital T), trauma and "small t", (as in lower case t), trauma.[8] Big T traumas are those events easily recognizable as traumatic, like abuse, combat, natural disasters, or major accidents. Not easily identified are the small "t" traumas. Many people overlook these small t traumas as unimportant and assume they should be able to "just get over it," if they themselves experienced the events or that children will not remember. They can include events like being laughed at, being picked on, moving from one house to another, hearing parents fight, dumping food on oneself at school resulting in embarrassment, or losing personal belongings, just to name a few. Both types of trauma can have lasting effects, as indicated by the participants' responses in the ACE's study. A frequent mistake parents or caregivers make is assuming that big T or small t events do not affect children because they are young. This belief could not be further from the truth. "Children are more vulnerable to trauma than adults,"[9] according to Dr. Bruce Perry because a traumatic event will alter an adult's original brain organization, but for a child, the event might be the brain's "original organizing experience."[10] Dr. Bessel Van der Kolk says that trauma is "unbearable and intolerable."[11] Dr. Van der Kolk states in his book, *The Body Keeps The Score*,[12] that everyone is affected by trauma either directly or indirectly through interactions and relationship with the traumatized person, or persons. Even after the danger has passed, the brainstem – responsible for survival- can be triggered when an individual senses danger. The "posttraumatic reactions" take over, and he or she feels as if the traumatic event is happening all over again at that moment, which leaves the person feeling helpless and out of control.[13]

"Children are more vulnerable to trauma than adults"
-Dr. Bruce Perry

Dr. Perry defines trauma as "an experience, or pattern of experiences, that impairs the proper functioning of the person's stress-response system, making it more reactive or sensitive", or events that are prolonged, overwhelming, and unpredictable.[14] "Trauma shocks the brain, stuns the mind, and freezes the body."[15] The possibilities of what the brain processes are vast considering these definitions. The small *t* trauma could include things like being locked in your room for crying, making a mistake like spilling milk, repeatedly being laughed at, being left in a car, saying the wrong answer in class, kids laughing at you for dropping your books, being left at home alone, or being forgotten at school long after everyone else has left. This list could go on and on. With repeated experiences like these, you may begin to feel that you do not fit with others, and you may internalize the message that you are not good enough, not worthy or not loveable.

Perhaps one of the most misunderstood aftermaths of trauma is the refusal of the experiences to fade into the past

Whether or not an experience is traumatic, meaning it causes lasting emotional, behavioral, or physiological problems, is different from one person to another. Every person perceives events differently based on his or her personality and life experiences, including all early childhood and family experiences. Therapists ask questions about childhood experiences when working with new clients to understand his or her perception of past events. If your family provided consistent, loving, and nurturing care when you were young and if they celebrated you and your accomplishments, chances are you will be better able to recover from bad experiences. If your family was chaotic and disorganized, ignored you, hurt you, made fun of you, or did not notice you or your accomplishments, chances are you will have difficulty handling bad experiences due to an inner belief of being inadequate, wrong, less valuable, and self-blaming. Everyone has had bad experiences. How a person internalizes those experiences makes the difference in whether the experience becomes a traumatic memory. It is essential to be able to learn from those experiences, understand how the brain processes those experiences, and learn how to take care of yourself when they occur.

Besides the anger, fear, sadness, nightmares, poor school and work performance, failed relationships, and physical illnesses mentioned in the introduction, there can be personal, internal patterns of thoughts and feelings that can be an aftermath of trauma. These patterns can include negative self-talk; an inability to see other people and experiences positively or even objectively –

Trauma Glasses; unrelenting reminders of the awful things that happened – Magnet Moments; feeling divided into parts that are stuck in the past- Parts; or deep-seated negative beliefs about oneself – Core Beliefs.

Perhaps one of the most misunderstood aftermaths of trauma is the refusal of the experiences to fade into the past. I do not remember whether I liked strained peas as an infant because that has disappeared into the haze of my past. I do remember how terrified I was when a skillet of grease caught fire while I was eating tomato soup. I was three years old; my mother was in the back of the house getting my brother ready to go to kindergarten, and I was alone in the kitchen when flames shot to the ceiling. I remember running down the hall screaming, unable to speak; unable to tell my mother what happened. My mom kept asking, "What's wrong, what's wrong," and I could not answer. To this day I do not like tomato soup. Maybe that is because of the grease fire; maybe my brain made a fearful association between tomato soup and fire, so now I believe tomato soup tastes nasty. The point is that early childhood experiences, even birth experiences, may not be entirely faded into the past.

3

IT'S NOT REALLY IN THE PAST

> *"When we feel threatened, or a possibility of injury, we draw from a library of possible responses"*
> —PETER LEVINE

It's dark. I don't know where I am. My chest hurts, I can't breathe, and all I know is I want my Mom. I want my Mom. I want my Mom. I want my Mom. Where is she? I want my Mom. My chest hurts. I can't breathe. Why doesn't she come? I want her. I want to scream for her, but I can't talk. All I can do is cry. I cry great wracking sobs and still she doesn't come. I cry and cry. I sob and scream, but she doesn't come. No one comes. No one comes. No one comes. It's dark. My chest hurts. I can't breathe.

It's quiet. It's dark. I might be asleep.

Quiet.

Dark.

Calm. I might be asleep.

My chest hurts. I want my Mom. Quiet. Calm. I want my Mom. My chest hurts. What is this place? Screaming. Great wracking sobs. Crying is all I can do, and she doesn't come. I want my Mom. I want my Mom. I want my Mom. I want my Mom.

Who are these other people? Not my Mom. I don't want them.

Quiet, calm. I must be sleeping.

It's her!!! There she is!!! It's Her!!! Mom. Mom. Mom. Mom.

Hold me.

Hold me.

Hold me.

Hold me. Never let me go.

That is not the story of a kidnapped child. That is my birth story. When I was born, I had fluid in my lungs and was in an incubator for a few days. I was not told that part of my birth story until I was an adult. Probably my parents thought it didn't matter since I was an infant, I lived to grow into a healthy child, and a healthy adult. No one would expect me to remember that because I did not have a verbal, narrative memory of it, yet all my life and continuing now, when I feel anxious, scared, or lonely, my chest hurts. My body remembers it. I recovered the emotional memory during a session of body-based therapy that led to the recovery and expression of emotional memories stored in my body. Later, doing EMDR therapy, I again felt the chest pain as well as the intense fear I felt during a recurring nightmare I used to have around age two.

Babies don't remember is a false assumption. The memories may be non-verbal and stored in the body-mind system. Memories of painful, unpleasant experiences can be stored in an unprocessed, frozen state, so that the negative emotions, negative thoughts, and even physical sensations feel as if the event just happened;

meaning the memory of the event is not really in the past regardless of how long ago it may have occurred. Non-verbal memories can be emotional and/or physical. My body remembered the pain of fluid in my lungs and the sad, frightening separation from my mother just after my birth.

"You should be over that by now"

Often, we tell ourselves, or others say to us, "you should be over that by now." When you hear the words *should* or *ought*, the rest of the statement will not be helpful. *Should* is an attempt to pretend something that is, isn't. It means we did something wrong or did not do something. Absolute words such as *should, always, have to*, and *must* are not helpful when dealing with human emotions. When you hear, "You shouldn't be angry about that," you probably feel even more angry. The truth is you are feeling angry. "You should be over that by now" means you are not over it yet. Memory storage and the significance of the event can determine whether the event continues to cause distress. Strained peas didn't matter but being separated from my mother did. Dr. Candace Pert stated that, "the body is the unconscious mind."[16] Our bodies do remember, and babies do remember! Ongoing distress about past experiences does not mean that something is wrong with you. It means you need to heal the emotional wounds.

Ongoing distress about past experiences does not mean that something is wrong with you. It means you need to heal the emotional wounds

Prince Harry

Most everyone can remember seeing video footage or photos of England's Prince William and his younger brother Prince Harry walking behind the horse-drawn coffin of their mother, Princess Diana. The Princess had died in a car crash and though Prince Harry was only 12 years old at the time, he complied with British custom, walking along behind his mother's coffin during the funeral service, with the entire world watching. The expressions on both the Princes' faces were heart-wrenching. The world watched both princes grow up, and the tabloids seemed to be delighted when Prince Harry got into trouble as a young man. He partied, he drank, and he was photographed naked with a young woman. There was no sympathetic reporting of the impact his mother's death had on him, just sensational, scandalous reporting. Twenty years later he began talking about it publicly, admitting he had been angry and tried to shut down his emotions.

Prince Harry recently disclosed that he sought counseling nearly twenty years after his mother's death. He said he had tried to avoid dealing with her death by refusing to think or talk about it. Prince Harry explained that he "shut down all his emotions,"[17] until he realized he was extremely angry, angry enough to want to punch someone. Prince Harry said he often felt he was having, or struggled with, the flight or fight response during official royal engagements. He stated, "I can safely say that losing my mum at the age of 12, and therefore shutting down all of my emotions for the last 20 years has had a quite serious effect on not only my personal life but my work as well. I have probably been very close to a complete breakdown on numerous occasions when all sorts of grief and sort of lies and misconceptions and everything is coming to you from every angle."[18] Prince Harry said that others, including his brother, encouraged him to seek help to deal with his emotions.

He said, "I know there is huge merit in talking about your issues and the only thing about keeping it quiet is that it's only ever going to make it worse."[19]

Prince Harry was honest about the consequences of his attempts to ignore and shut down the impact of his mother's death. Among the things he has not talked about publicly are his core beliefs about himself and how they may have changed when his mother died. His mother reportedly believed "Harry's the naughty one, just like me."[20] She might have taught him that belief; we will never know. We do know that core beliefs start forming very early in a child's life and have a lasting impact, possibly creating significant obstacles to healing past traumatic memories.

Core beliefs start forming very early in a child's life and have a lasting impact, possibly creating significant obstacles to healing past traumatic memories

4

BELIEFS ARE THE CORE

"I know what it's like to be afraid of your own mind"
-UNKNOWN

Babies are not born with a preset belief system. The belief system starts forming in infancy and continues throughout life. Beliefs are shaped by how we interact with others in our world, such as parents, siblings, grandparents, teachers, and peers in our immediate circle. Beliefs can be formed by what we read, see, and hear. We form beliefs about ourselves, about others, about the world, about what the future will be, and how we fit into the world. Babies and children believe the messages they get from the adults around them. They are developmentally incapable of evaluating whether a message is true or false, so they internalize all messages as true. These early beliefs create the framework against which all incoming information is compared. Beliefs are powerful because we live our lives from them, whether they are positive or negative, true, or false. Beliefs are important because they form the stories we tell ourselves about who we are, what we do, what we can or cannot accomplish in life and how we compare ourselves with others.

What happens during those early years if parents are less than consistent, loving, and nurturing? According to Sigmund Freud, humans have two primary instinctual drives: sex and death.[21] Some of the theorists who came after Freud disagreed and said our most powerful drive is to connect with others. Current research in brain development and biology supports the importance of the theory of connection.[22] We are biologically hard-wired to be in relationship with other people. The need to be connected to others is strong enough that babies can die from lack of physical touch and connection. According to Object Relations theorists, who came after Freud, the need for an infant to connect to a caregiver and to experience the world as a safe place is strong. When parents or caregivers are absent, neglectful, abusive, or inconsistent, babies can sense at a deep, pre-verbal, non-verbal level that *there is something wrong/bad about me or they wouldn't treat me this way.* When parents are inconsistent a child's experience is that sometimes they get "good parent, and sometimes they get "bad parent," creating a rollercoaster of hope and disappointment. If a child could express his feelings, he might say something like:

"She did it again"
"No, she didn't"
"She's going to love me"
"Maybe today she will be nice"
"Maybe this time she will do what she said"

Babies and toddlers can only perceive the world from their own perspective. By design and function of the brain, children are egocentric. They believe they are the center of the universe, that everything is about them. They believe they are the cause of all that happens, good or bad. Notice what happens when a baby is present; all eyes, and attention, are on the baby. When this attention is positive, it begins to lay the foundation for healthy self-esteem and self-worth. The actions and words of caregivers serve as a mirror for young children, reflecting their worth and value. When a parent notices and applauds a child's accomplishment, whether the child is crawling, standing up, getting a hit in baseball, sharing a toy, reading for himself or taking his dish to the sink, the real message parents communicate is "you are worth my time and attention." It is important that parents spend quality time with their children, go to ball games, recitals, school plays, and teacher conferences. It helps children learn that "I matter." Conversely, if parents are too busy, too depressed, or too absorbed in their own activities to notice what their children are doing, the real message learned is "I am not worth my parents' time. I don't matter."

Do you know what *your* core beliefs are? Sometimes we don't know until an event brings them to the surface or we purposely reflect on them. How you spend your time and your actions and behaviors are a clue to what your core beliefs are. The comments you remember your parents/grandparents making is another clue. The things we remember most from childhood are the things that have an emotional charge to them, whether positive or negative. We can all recall where we were on 9/11/2001 when the planes hit the World Trade Center buildings and the Pentagon because of the emotional charge of that day. If you are old enough, you remember the assassination of President John F. Kennedy and where you were that day. Often parents have no idea the emotional impact or the lasting effect their comments and behaviors may have on their children. By observing parents, children develop unspoken beliefs about what men are like, what women are like, how men and women treat each other, how they (children) should act, and can expect to be treated. Here is an example:

Susan's childhood piano teacher said it was okay for girls to major in music because they would have a husband to take care of them, but boys should not, because boys would need to support a family. That belief did not "take" with her because from her earliest memory, her parents talked about "when" she would go to college, not "if." Her father told her it was important to be able to take care of herself, and not depend on a man/husband to support her. That was in the 1950s and 1960s, and while her father wasn't necessarily a feminist ahead of his time, his own father died in 1928 when he was just eight years old. After that, his mother ran a print shop to support her children. From that experience, Susan's father developed a core belief about the importance of women's self-reliance, and imparted that belief to Susan, which in turn became a core belief for her.

Another example is Jules, a professional colleague, and an EMDR trained therapist. Jules knew she had a challenging relationship with her mother, but never knew why. She said that there were years when there was constant conflict and tension between the two of them. Jules stated her core beliefs were that she was just not good enough and was not lovable. She had heard stories about experiences from her infancy and childhood, and then realized through EMDR therapy that she had no attachment or bond with her mother. Even when her mother would feed her as an infant, there was no connection to her. The lack of attachment and bond with her mom left her with the core belief that something was wrong with her, which created challenges with most all her relationships, including the relationships with her own children.

What parents do and say matters. For you to begin uncovering what core beliefs you may have developed, consider the following questions:

What messages did you get from your parents?

Did you have a nickname? Was it a kind nickname?

Did your parents groan and complain when you asked for or needed something?

Did they yell at you?

Did they notice you?

Did they applaud you? How did you feel when they did?

Common negative core beliefs may include the following (but not limited to):

> *I'm not good enough*
> *I don't matter*
> *I'm not lovable*
> *It's my fault*
> *I'm not safe*
> *I'm helpless*
> *I can't*
> *I can't trust anyone*
> *I can't trust myself*
> *I must earn the right to exist*
> *I must be perfect*
> *I must have done something wrong*
> *I should have done something differently*

If reading the list stirred some emotions in you, it may be a sign that you hold some negative core beliefs. If you hold these beliefs outside of your conscious awareness, they will work on you in unconscious ways. Several years ago, a 30-something-year-old woman, who was sexually abused when she was three years old, said to me "I must have done something to cause it...," and she believed that. My response was "that's not possible." Do you believe a three-year-old can cause sexual abuse? A belief that you are at fault, for all the bad things in your life, will lead you to feel guilty, overly responsible, and ashamed, if not lead to outright self-hatred. Here is another list of possible core beliefs:

I am worthy
I have value
I am beautiful
I deserve good things
I am lovable
I am powerful
I do my best
I am okay
I can

If you read this list and your mind says, "Yeah, I know that, but it doesn't feel true," or your mind says, "I have never felt that way," or if those things are hard to say out loud you probably have negative core beliefs. Regardless, whether you have one or a set of negative core beliefs, they can block you from having the life you want.

Most of us, even if we had loving, nurturing parents, have some negative core beliefs. Even parents with the best of intentions can teach negative beliefs without ever meaning to or knowing they did. My mother grew up poor in rural Mississippi and lived through the Great Depression. My mother said she did not know they were poor, and she thought everyone lived the way they did. She remembered when her father lost everything, even their house, because the price of cotton fell before he had taken his crop to market. What belief did I absorb from parents who lived through the depression, a mother who grew up poor in Mississippi, and a father raised by a single mother who ran a print shop? I learned that work is good while money is bad, that you must work very hard to have money, it is important to be selfless, and not to ask for things that are extravagant.

Grape juice was extravagant. I loved grape juice as a child and remember asking when we could have some. The answer I remember was "when the price goes down." There was no criticism or anger in my parents' response, but I got the idea that asking for things that were expensive was not okay. To this day, I often struggle with guilt when I buy something I want, but don't need. I have spent most of my life working very hard for little money. My family was also quiet and did not openly express anger, so I did not learn to express anger or tolerate anger until adulthood. I still carry a basic need to have those around me be happy, get along, and like me. That need has set me up for difficulties. Albeit, compared to those who lived with abusive or neglectful parents, my negative beliefs are mild, I still have them, even having grown up with consistently loving, nurturing parents.

Negative beliefs limit life. They prevent a person from reaching his or her full potential in life – relationally, academically, or professionally. Most people tend to accept, reject, or alter new information, so that it fits within the beliefs formed in childhood. When PTSD and strong negative core beliefs are combined, the results can be personal misery and possibly personal injury.

Regardless, whether you have one or a set of negative core beliefs, they can block you from having the life you want

Out of Control Anxiety – Carrie

Carrie* came to therapy because her feelings of anxiety had gotten out of control. Answering questions in therapy sessions was nerve-wracking for her, and it took months for her to feel any degree of trust with me. She said her earliest memory was of her mother trying to kill her father when she was in the third grade. As her sessions unfolded, she described a childhood filled with criticism and physical, verbal, and emotional abuse in a rigid, intolerant religious setting. Her parents regularly told her that she needed to do better at everything. She went to a private, religious school where she was severely punished by her teachers for behaviors that were typical for her age. Her parents argued often, and their arguments frequently escalated to physical fights. She was sexually abused by an uncle and a neighborhood boy and was afraid to tell anyone. She did not have an escape or a safe place to go. At age 18, in keeping with her family's values, she started college at a Christian school where she was later kicked out for drinking.

Carrie's traumatic experiences continued into her adult life. Her husband was unfaithful, and they argued frequently. Their arguments consisted of bitter verbal attacks, throwing objects at each other, breaking objects, and threating each other. She had frequent thoughts of killing herself and finally took a handful of pills. A friend happened to find her and got help in time to save her life. She was hospitalized because of the suicide attempt, and then restrained by the hospital staff. Afterward, she did not trust anyone. Her husband taunted her for failing at killing herself. He threatened that if she tried to leave him, he would kill her and hide her body where no one would find her. She lived in a constant state of fear.

The year before starting therapy, police stormed her home in a case of mistaken identity. During the incident, an officer yelled at her and pointed a gun at her face. As a result, Carrie was terrified of police officers and would not consider calling them for help in any circumstance. She was on the brink of getting a divorce, and one of the ways she coped was to work. Work was a refuge, and she worked excessive hours. During the early months of therapy before she trusted me, did not disclose her suicidal thoughts. Nevertheless, she never missed a therapy session and did everything I suggested. Despite all she went through, or maybe because of what she went through, she is one of the most courageous people I have ever met.

Carrie lived with a set of core beliefs that made her miserable and moved her closer and closer to suicide. Here are some of her beliefs:

It's my fault
Nothing will ever get better
Death/suicide is inevitable
I should die
Anger is a sin
If I feel angry, I am bad, and should die
If I make a mistake, I am bad and should die

Carrie believed everything was her fault. Her parents argued about her, so that was her fault. It was her fault because she existed. The sexual abuse was her fault because she should have done something to prevent it or stop it. If anyone got mad at her, it was her fault. Her husband's infidelities meant she was not a good wife, so it was her fault. If she felt angry, that was a sin; it meant she was a bad person, so she should die. I told her more than once during therapy, "We're only working to change everything you believe." How daunting it must be to change everything you believe about your family, yourself, your responsibilities, what is right and wrong, whether God is a loving God or whether God hates you, whether you are destined to have bad things happen to you and kill yourself, and even whether it is possible to be happy.

As I said, Carrie is one of the most courageous people I know. She continues to work hard in therapy despite serious family issues like cancer, criminal charges, legal trials, and deaths. She has endured through continued arguments with her husband, despite boatloads of stupidity to deal with at work and despite wanting to die. Not only that, therapy is working. She no longer has violent, bloody nightmares every night. She no longer believes everything is her fault or that she should die if someone is mad at her. She has safe places she can visualize and calm herself and has ideas about what she wants in her life. She laughs about being on a fifteen-year therapy plan. Maybe it will be fifteen years, maybe not. We will continue until she gets where she wants to be. The hope for treatment is that Carrie develops positive core beliefs, so that she can feel good about and like herself. That she builds a life that feels satisfying, free of nightmares, fears, threats, and self-hatred, a life in which she has healed the various parts of herself, some of which are still stuck in the past. This can be a scary part of therapy for people; working on those parts that are stuck in the past, or even entertaining the idea that some parts of ourselves are stuck in the past. But the truth is we all have parts, so now let's talk about them.

5

PARTS OF YOU

> *"Without realizing it, I fought to keep my two worlds separated. Without ever knowing why, I made sure, whenever possible, that nothing passed between the compartmentalization I had created between the day child and the night child"*
>
> MARILYN VAN DERBUR

Everyone has parts of themselves. Even those of us with good mental and emotional health with few distressing events in our life have parts. We have parts that fill different roles, like a parent, spouse, sister, brother, employee, or supervisor. Most of us act differently depending on which role we are in, or what part is in charge at the moment. We all have our public and private face. We put on our "game face" when we go to work. When we get home, hopefully, we can put on our private face where we can relax, be more casual, and entirely be ourselves. Under stress, however, most of us regress to less effective, less favorable, often younger acting behaviors. To use our best, most effective behaviors, we need to feel safe, secure, calm, and confident.

In addition to the role parts, we have emotional parts. For example, we have the excited part when seeing family and friends, the happy part, the overjoyed part, the satisfied part

There can also be negative parts that that get angry, the part that doesn't trust, the part that feels scared, the part that feels sad, the part that wants to cry, and the part that just wants to run away. We can even have parts that are younger than our current chronological age. Not long ago, I discovered I have a young part, maybe about five-years-old, that doesn't want to be a grown up and doesn't want to go to work. On Monday mornings, or when there is a lot of stress at the office, my younger part wants to take charge. When this happens, I have a hard day at work. I can get sad, cranky, irritable, and unmotivated. That's when I know I need to play to take care of my five-year-old. That's also when I tend to miss my parents. Remember, five-year-old's have parents to take care of them and handle problems for them.

Having "parts" does not mean you are crazy. We all have parts. If your parts sometimes take control or if you have periods of time you don't remember, it could mean you have monsters in the bottom drawer that need healing (more about this later). If you have a sense that you do have "parts," be aware they are always listening; they are part of you and have a job to do. Their job is to protect you. The parts may know things that you don't remember; they may be very young, and not know that you are an adult and able to handle things they couldn't have managed. They still need the things they didn't get when they were young and got overwhelmed. Children need to be noticed, loved, nurtured, celebrated, cared for, and kept safe. Someone who has young parts and has gradually become aware of them is Ellen.

Terrible Childhood – Ellen

Ellen* had what any person would describe as a horrific childhood. Both her parents were abusive to her and favored her siblings. Her mother was physically abusive from the time Ellen was about six years old. The abuse appeared intentional and vicious, and entirely unpredictable to Ellen. Her mother would wake her up to beat her; she slammed her head on a tile floor in the bathroom because water spilled on the floor, and she threatened Ellen with a variety of weapons. Her mother went out of her way to make all holidays and birthdays miserable, giving Ellen gifts and then breaking them in front of her. Her father was equally verbally abusive and coercive. He forced Ellen to drown a litter of kittens when she was young without ever explaining the reason why. He killed her favorite pet. At times she was not allowed to eat. At other times, her mother intentionally forced her to eat foods she was allergic to knowing she would become very ill.

Both of her parents showed marked favoritism toward Ellen's siblings by buying clothes and gifts for them, but not for Ellen. If Ellen showed any emotion, her parents would beat her. Ellen learned at a very young age that there was no safe place for her in the family. She was afraid to sleep for fear of what might happen to her. She learned to stuff all her emotions and expected no help from her parents. She was criticized for doing well in school and making her siblings feel bad because her grades were better than theirs. When she noticed that her friend's family was kind, loving, and enjoyed being together, it made her truly recognize just how bad her home was. She knew her only way to survive was to get out as soon as she could.

When she finally left home, Ellen cut off all contact with her parents. After that, her father came to her workplace and her home threatening to kill her. He broke into her home during the middle of the night. The result for Ellen was near constant anxiety and fear for her safety, frequent nightmares, flashbacks, depression, and difficulty sleeping. Even though she left home, her past followed her. She disliked holidays and did not celebrate them. Sometimes she would blank out and lose track of time. When she started therapy, the memory of her father breaking into her home was so vague she was unsure whether it really happened. She had many memories to work through to heal. Despite all that she successfully held a professional level job.

Not only did Ellen have many state-level memories, but she also had parts. It took several weeks of therapy to discover the parts. She agreed to begin EMDR therapy and right away began listing the past experiences that were disturbing to her and putting disturbance ratings on them. During her EMDR processing sessions, she felt physical sensations like tightness in her muscles, headaches, or sometimes nausea. She noticed her feelings shift from fear to sadness to anger. Anger was helpful for her. It helped her feel empowered, and it was a natural consequence of recognizing just how poorly and unfairly she had been treated. Several sessions into her EMDR processing she noticed that when she felt afraid or sad, a part of her also felt as young as five or six. These young parts held different feelings of sadness, anger, and resentment and not all the parts were ready for processing her childhood experiences. As she continued with therapy, her memories started to become less hazy, and she began to feel safe. She also adopted a dog, started yoga classes, and using relaxation apps on her phone. Not all of therapy happens in the therapist's office. Everything Ellen began to do was helping her heal. After about six months of therapy, Ellen's symptoms of PTSD decreased significantly. She felt more confident, especially about ending contact with her family. She finally felt safer at home, felt less anxiety and depression, was making plans for a vacation, and was continuing therapy because she realized that therapy was working to help her have the life she wanted.

6

THE MONSTERS IN THE BOTTOM DRAWER

"After a traumatic experience, the human system of self-preservation seems to go on permanent alert, as if the danger might return at any moment"

−UNKNOWN

Several times we have mentioned bottom drawer memories. Memories that are stuffed deep down in the brain are called state-level memories and it all comes down to understanding the brain and how it works. According to Dr. Bruce Perry,[23] it is necessary to understand memory to understand trauma.[24] Dr. Perry talks about the four levels of memory in the brain – like a four-drawer filing cabinet. The first level of memory or top drawer of the file cabinet is *cognitive memory*. It is connected to the cerebral cortex and is information that it is easily accessible and non-emotional.

Examples of cognitive memory, or the conscious mind, are what you had for breakfast, what kind of car you drive, the name of the book you are reading, the names of presidents, and much of what you learned in school. Neuroscientists call this explicit or declarative memory.

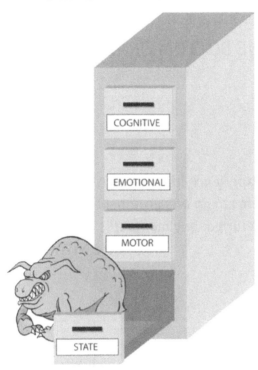

TRAUMA and MEMORY

Trauma is buried at the state level; which directs all other responses.
© Beyond Consequences Institute, LLC, used with permission

The second level of memory, or second drawer, in the file cabinet is *emotional memory*. It is connected to the limbic system and consists of the feelings evoked by an experience or a memory. Think back to high school and the name of someone you knew. In addition to the cognitive memory from the first drawer you may also notice that you have a feeling about that person either positive or negative depending on how you felt about them. That is an example of the cognitive and emotional drawer connection. If you see your first-grade teacher in the grocery store you might get a warm, happy feeling or you might feel tense, angry, afraid, and duck around to the next aisle depending on how you felt about the teacher. The feelings that come up are emotional memories.

The third level of memory, or third drawer of the file cabinet, is motor or procedural memory; also called non-declarative memory. Have you ever gotten on a bike after some years and just started peddling? That is muscle memory. Musicians and athletes practice to develop muscle memory. Baseball players do not consciously think how hard to grip the bat, or how to shift their weight when they swing at pitches during games. Their body knows what to do because they have built muscle memory through practice. A pianist does not have to consciously think about which fingers go to which keys or how hard to push the keys. Practice has taught the pianist what to do without the need for conscious thought.

The fourth level of memory, or bottom drawer of the file cabinet, is the state-level memory, it is stored close to the brainstem, which is called the primitive brain. The state-level drawer is where distressing or traumatic memories are stored, sometimes entirely outside conscious awareness, and sometimes in fragments. Attached to these state-level memories are the sensations the person saw, heard, tasted, touched, or smelled when the event happened.[25]

Unexpected triggers can activate state-level memories and create physical, behavioral, or emotional reactions that make the individual appear out of control. It's like a monster came out of the drawer. These memories are referred to as "state-level" because they were created in an extreme emotional state.[26] When the memories are triggered, that state can be re-created, all at a subconscious level of awareness. An example is in the television show West Wing;[27] there was a shooting in one episode resulting in injuries to President Bartlett, and some of his staff. Months later one of the staff started having unexplained emotional reactions when hearing Christmas music played in the White House. A psychologist helped him realize that the sound of Christmas bells was triggering memories of the sounds of the ambulances after the shooting.

Following are some client examples of memory triggers from state-level drawers of some of our clients. A young man who grew up in a home with parents who often fought violently once came home from school on a grey, cloudy day wearing sweaty football pads and walked in on a fight between his parents. Months, and even years later, he would get upset by the smell of sweaty football pads. Another example is of a young woman who felt sad and depressed every year in the fall. She could not explain why she felt that way, but her life included several traumatic events that all happened in November. Jules from Chapter 4 reported needing something with sugar each time she felt anxious or stressed. The sugar appeared to calm her down. She knew her mother added sugar to her formula, so Jules finally recognized that she had made a connection with the sugary formula instead of with her mother. So, when she felt stressed and anxious, she sought her first source of comfort –sweet, sugary foods. Knowledge about the levels of memory clarifies how the memories are stored and in choosing the right therapeutic approach to heal memories.

Recent brain research has demonstrated that the amygdala, the alarm system in the brain, can trigger emotions and physical reactions before signals get to the cortex where thinking happens. Due to the way memories are stored in the brain, and the way the brain handles sensory input, it most likely is not possible to "think" yourself out of an emotional reaction to a situation or to talk yourself out of feeling anxious, afraid, sad, or angry, or any other emotion. Traditional talk therapy that works only at the cognitive, or cortex, level of memory will not get to the level of body/muscle memory, or the state-level memory. According to Dr. William Steele, traumatic memories are more easily communicated through images and sensory activities than through cognitive processes.[28] Accessing in order to heal state-level memories is not a cognitive-level drawer, or thinking, process. The state-level drawer must be accessed to heal state-level memories.

Healing state level memories requires facing the monsters

This next example is a person with a story that sounds like a horror movie, but the story is true. She had a multitude of monsters in the bottom drawer, and she dissociated to protect herself. Dissociation can be a protective mechanism when a person is experiencing extreme, repeated abuse. If you can't get away from, stop, or change the abuse and have no choice except to endure it, your mind might decide, "I'm out of here." Your mind might go somewhere else, so you don't have to experience the pain, horror, or terror of what is happening. During her episodes of abuse, Cameron's mind checked out, took her somewhere else to spare her the pain, terror, and revulsion about what was happening to her. Her recovery through EMDR therapy was as powerful as her history was horrifying. Here is her story.

Prince Charming Hyde (as in Jekyll and Hyde)

Cameron* was raised in a well-to-do family in California. She moved to the Midwest in her teens. Being the new girl in a new school was daunting for her since she was more of an introvert and trying to fit in with well-established groups in the high school she attended was not easy. Her parents were loving, caring, nurturing, and available for her. By her account, she had a charmed life. Then she met a boy in high school who was a grade ahead of her. He was a tall, handsome, popular football player, and was kind to her.

Cameron thought she had met her Prince Charming. They dated for almost two years before getting married. She had a fairy-tale wedding, a month-long honeymoon in Europe, and a fairy-tale idea of what her married life was going to be. The fairy-tale did not last long.

When they arrived at their hotel in Paris, her husband was rude and ignored her. She thought it must have been due to exhaustion from wedding preparations and a long overseas flight. Her first sexual experience was on her wedding night. It dashed her hopes about what their first time would be. He was harsh, cruel, and caused her a tremendous amount of pain. She had trouble walking the next morning. He had no empathy for her and yelled at her. He was angry that she could not go sightseeing. He told her she was faking the pain and she was a spoiled brat. She forced herself to get ready for the day because she was supposed to honor her husband. During the day of sightseeing he walked ahead of her as if he were embarrassed, he offered her no assistance, did not wait for her, nor get her food or water. She had no frame-of-reference for this type of treatment and was totally confused by his switch in personality.

For the rest of the honeymoon her husband treated her the same way. He did not say a kind word to her the entire time. He disregarded her physical well-being, was sexually aggressive, called her hateful, ugly names, and treated her horribly. His kindness towards her while they were dating, compared to his severe maltreatment of her since their wedding made him appear like Dr. Jekyll and Mr. Hyde. Cameron was scared and did not know what to do. She was afraid to tell her parents, so she bottled it up and pretended it was not happening.

Cameron came to therapy after her divorce. She had been married for 12 years and had two children, a boy and a girl, during the marriage. She had endured horrific torture all those years. She told the story of her marriage and the abusive treatment by her husband as if she were reading from the telephone book – no emotion, no connection to how horrible her story was, no feelings at all. She told how the things that happened on the honeymoon continued daily throughout their marriage and got even worse. He called her horrible names and degraded her for everything she did around the house, to the point she felt she could do nothing. His physical abuse turned into life-threatening torture. The only way she endured was to dissociate; she would go to another place in her mind to escape the pain and terror. She was too afraid to tell anyone because he threatened to kill her, their children, and her family if she ever said anything. She endured this treatment for 12 years until he physically hurt their daughter.

Earlier examples of state-level memories were from people's childhoods. In Cameron's case, her childhood memories were happy ones, so the monsters in her state-level drawer were from her adult life. At the beginning of her therapy, we compared Cameron's state-level memories to an inflated balloon. The balloon represented the memories themselves. The air that inflated the balloon consisted of the sensations she had during the abusive experiences – what she saw, heard, felt, smelt, or tasted. The goal of her therapy was to deflate each of the balloons. The memory, or balloon, would still be there, Cameron would just not have any feelings about the memories; nor could the balloon be re-inflated. We started with EMDR Therapy to begin healing the memories of those 12 years. First, we made sure she had resources to rely on during this process, so that working through the memories would not overwhelm her and cause her to dissociate during therapy. The resources she chose were her family, especially her mother. Once she had resources in place, we began the trauma reprocessing by revisiting her memories. She started with the honeymoon memories. She was able to mentally confront her ex-husband in the reprocessing by telling him how she felt about what he did to her and visualize bringing in her father to protect her from the abuse she experienced.

Therapy took time for her to clear out her state-level drawer because she had been conditioned to believe what her ex-husband said about her. We went back to the memories that had significance for her and allowed her parts to tell what they needed to tell. She healed the memories by mentally visualizing confronting her husband and seeing herself for who she was, not who her husband had said she was. There were times when she imagined bringing other people into the memory to help her heal. Her childhood belief system had given way to the belief system of her husband. She believed she deserved the way he treated her, that she was incompetent in every way, and that her only purpose in life was to be a sex slave for him. It took time for her to be able to step back and see the memories differently, to understand that the problem was him, not her, and to know that he was not a good person. Because of the hard work she did in therapy, Cameron is doing well, her children are well, and she is venturing into a new relationship. She did the work to overcome the memories of what her ex-husband did to her. The memories are still there, but now she does not become upset about them. She can walk confidently into her new life knowing that the abuse she endured will not negatively impact her life ever again.

7

HOW DID YOUR BRAIN GET THIS WAY

> *"Childhood trauma does not come in one single package"*
>
> –ASA DON BROWN

Next, we are going to get a bit academic and share some basic information about brain development, how early experiences affect brain development, and what parts of the brain-guide us in different emotional states.

> **"Children's early experiences shape their whole life trajectories"**
>
> –K. Sukel

The first three years of life are a critical time for brain development. The foundation of emotional health is formed during those years and babies are doing much more than eating, sleeping, crying, and pooping. They are developing a sense of whether the world is a safe place, whether they can trust, whether they have value, and this is all happening at a pre/non-verbal level. According to Dr. Bruce Perry, the brain is a pattern seeking muscle whose development depends on experience.[29] "Children's early experiences shape their whole life trajectories. Even experiences before birth, the conditions that the mother lives in while she's pregnant, have an influence on a baby's development. You don't have to be a neuroscientist to know that these factors can influence one's whole life."[30] Every experience, from birth forward, is stored in the subconscious brain and a person will live by those stored patterns, habits, and beliefs. Just as bodies require water and food to grow, brains need positive experiences to grow in healthy ways.

Babies cry. At one time we were all babies that cried. Babies cry when they are hungry, scared, lonely, hot, cold, or wet. They will start with some restlessness, a whimper, then begin to cry, and then go to a full-out wail if a caring adult has not answered the cry. Ideally, a parent, or caregiver, notices what a baby needs and somewhere between the whimper and the full-out wail, will come to meet the need in a calm, nurturing way, and the baby begins to build trust. When this happens repeatedly, babies gain a sense that someone will meet their needs and the world is a safe place. Propping a bottle in a baby's mouth and walking away does not meet a baby's emotional and physical needs. Turning on the television during feeding, without interacting with the baby does not build attachment. Meeting the need means picking the baby up, rocking, talking, cooing, singing, and touching. These actions are called motherese and help a baby develop core beliefs during the first years of life that she is safe, that she is worth being taken care of, has value, and that she can trust. A sense of self-worth is being created based on these early interactions and patterns of experiences with caregivers.

The brain and body store these experiences in every cell of the body.[31] Brain development happens in a set sequence; neurosequentially from bottom to top, and the function of the brain is hierarchical.[32] If something goes amiss with the development of the lower parts of the brain that develop first, the higher-level parts of the brain will not function optimally.[33] It's like math - if a child does not learn to add and subtract then multiplication and division will be tough, if not impossible without some corrective intervention for the brain to acquire the necessary skills.

Next is a quick look at some basic structures of the brain that will be important in understanding how the brain stores memories of distressing events. This description is a very brief, simplified summary of the brainstem, limbic system, amygdala, hippocampus, and the cerebral cortex.

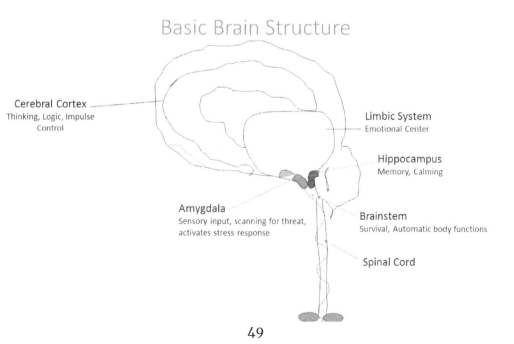

Brainstem

The brainstem connects to the spinal cord and relays information between the brain and the body. It is responsible for basic survival, controlling automatic body functions that we do not think about like consciousness, heart rate, breathing, digestion, body temperature, physical coordination, and wake-sleep cycles. The brainstem is the non-thinking, primitive part of the brain.

Limbic System

Emotions drive us and the Limbic System is the emotional center of the brain. According to Dr. Bessel van der Kolk, "It is the seat of the emotions, the monitor of danger, the judge of what is pleasurable or scary, the arbiter of what is or is not important for survival purposes."[34] It is a sophisticated collection of structures responsible for different aspects of emotions and the formation of memories. The amygdala and hippocampus are part of the limbic system as well as the thalamus, hypothalamus, basal ganglia, and cingulate gyrus. Its functions include short and long-term memory, motivation, behaviors, attachment to others, mood, emotions, and empathy. The limbic system is emotional. When feelings become extreme, whether we feel afraid, sad, shocked, or upset, we sink into our limbic system, and our ability to think, respond, speak, or even hear can shut down.[35]

For example, when a child is in the midst of a full-blown temper tantrum, adults might say things like:

"You need to calm down"
"Go to your room"
"If you keep doing that, you will be in trouble"
"You have no reason to be upset right now"

"If you keep crying, I will give you something to cry about"

Comments like those can literally fall on deaf ears or sound like a threat to a child. In the midst of a tantrum, his limbic system may have taken over and shut down the cortex, leaving him unable to listen, think, or calm down. The same thing can happen with adults, for example, when a doctor gives terrible news. Often people say, "The doctor told me I have cancer and I don't remember anything after that." This memory fog happens when emotions become extreme and shut down the higher areas of the brain. Dr. Bruce Perry has explained that when we perceive threat or danger, our state of emotional arousal moves from a state of calm, to alert, to alarm, to fear, and finally to terror.[36] (see Image A, page 93) As our emotional arousal moves toward threat, the part of our brain that manages our behaviors moves down from the higher levels of the brain to the lower, more primitive areas of the brain. In a state of abject terror, we operate out of instinct from our brainstem.

Amygdala

The amygdala is deep in the center of the limbic system, about the size and shape of an almond, and it is always on alert. It works with the hippocampus to produce emotions and is the brain's alarm system. The amygdala is fully operational at birth and does not think. Its job is to scan the environment for threat, receive sensory input, then route the sensory information to other parts of the brain. When the amygdala senses threat, (and it decides what is or is not a threat), it will activate the body's stress response system. Our stress response system prepares the body to freeze, run away, fight, or in the most severe cases faint. The amygdala can send alarm signals to the body that create a physical reaction before any messages get to the thinking part of the brain. Feelings of fear or anxiety with sensations like rapid heart rate, rapid breathing, tense muscles, sweaty palms, or stomach aches can be the result of the amygdala sending alarm signals to the body. When a person experiences repeated frightening experiences, especially when very young, the amygdala can become over-active. It can get stuck in the "on position." Some children and adults live continuously at a higher stress level, which could be the result of the over-activated amygdala.

Hippocampus

Another small structure near the brainstem and amygdala is the hippocampus. It resembles a seahorse and is in two parts on each side of the brain, under the cerebral cortex. The hippocampus is involved in processing information and new experiences for both short-term and long-term memory storage. It can also calm the stress response system when the amygdala sounds an alarm. But, the hippocampus does not come entirely online, fully functional, until a person is about three-years-old, meaning an infant is not able to calm herself down when upset.[37] She needs an adult to provide a nurturing and soothing response when stressed. Leaving a baby alone to "cry it out," on the other hand, is harmful to healthy brain development! Babies who are ignored and left alone learn that the world is not safe, adults will not care for them, and they are not worthy of care. Eventually, ignored babies will stop crying, which is a bad sign; it means they have given up waiting for someone to care for them. They have stored a brain pattern that people are not trustworthy, the world is not a safe place, and they will have to take care of themselves.

	Calm	Alert	Alarm	Fear	Terror
Regulating Brain Region	Neocortex Cortex	Cortex Limbic	Limbic Midbrain	Midbrain Brainstem	Brainstem Autonomic
Cognition	Abstract	Concrete	Emotional	Reactive	Reflexive
Hyper-arousal		Vigilance	Resistance	Defiance	Aggression
Dissociative		Avoidance	Compliance	Dissociation	Fainting
Escalating Behaviors (behaviors of care-givers/teachers that escalate the state of arousal)	Talking Poking Noise Television	Frustration Anxiety Communicating from a distance without eye contact Complex directions Ultimatums	Raised voice Raised hand Shaking finger Yelling Threats Chaos	Increased or continued frustration Yelling Chaos Sense of fear	Inappropriate physical restraint Grabbing Shaking Screaming
De-escalating behaviors (behaviors of care-givers/teachers that calm the state of arousal)	Presence Quiet Rocking	Quiet voice Eye contact Confidence Clear, simple directives	Slow, sure physical touch "Invited" touch Quiet, melodic words Singing Humming Music	Presence Quiet Confidence Disengagement	Appropriate physical restraint Withdrawal from class TIME

States of Emotional Arousal Adapted from Dr. Bruce Perry All Rights Reserved © 2017-2018 Bruce D. Perry

Cerebral Cortex

The cerebral cortex is the outer layer of the brain and makes up about 40% of the entire brain. It is responsible for higher-level brain functions including rational thought, logic, decision-making, attention, awareness, cognition, language, intelligence, voluntary physical actions, and consequential thinking. These abilities are known as executive functions and develop gradually throughout childhood and adolescence. The cerebral cortex has four sections, or lobes: the frontal lobe, the parietal lobe, the occipital lobe, and temporal lobe. The cerebral cortex is what makes us human and separates us from other mammals. Research has shown that the frontal lobe of the cerebral cortex continues to develop until about age 25 for females and 28 for males.[38] The pre-frontal cortex is the center for thinking, logic, and impulse control. This is the part of the brain that allows us to think before we act on an impulse, to delay gratification, to "act like an adult" and be our best self. When we are in a calm emotional state, we can use our pre-frontal cortex to make decisions based on logic, lists of pros and cons, and what our better judgment tells us is good to do or not to do.

Because they influence the way we interact with others, understanding our own core beliefs is essential (discussed in Ch. 3). With understanding and practice, it is possible to become aware of your core beliefs, what emotional state you are in, and what part of your brain is driving you. Without understanding and practice, most of us shift unconsciously out of our cortex and into our limbic system or even our brain stem when we become upset. That is what happens when panic attacks seem to come out of the blue, for no reason. Olivia is one of the people who said precisely that about her first panic attack. As panic attacks do, hers became more frequent until she was unable to do many of the things she used to do and wanted to do.

Life Changes - Olivia

Olivia* started therapy when her husband's prolonged health problems caused a change in his ability to relate to her emotionally. He quit communicating, he stopped showing affection, and he told her to "get a life." That may not seem like the starting place to work on childhood abuse, but it was. When her husband changed, Olivia's anxiety came back even though she had previously worked on anxiety with a different therapist, using a cognitive-based therapy. Olivia had a history of anxiety and panic attacks with her first panic attack occurring years earlier during a long drive to move closer to her mother.

When Olivia was a child, her mother was verbally and physically abusive to her. She locked Olivia in dark closets and gave her unnecessary enemas. In a home where she felt unimportant, unsafe, and invisible, sucking her thumb was the one coping skill she had to help her feel a bit of safety and comfort. Her mother took that away from Olivia by taping her thumb. When she was four years old, her mother put duct tape with hot sauce and chili powder on her thumb and sent her to bed alone. When she was eleven years old she learned to drive, so that she could drive herself to work as a babysitter. For her, driving was a chore, a task, something else for her to do alone, and not the new privilege it is for most teenagers. Then when she was seventeen years old, her father died. At the time of his death she was ignored, left alone, and offered no comfort from her mother or other family members. She was then expected to make his funeral arrangements, which she did.

Experiences that increased her sense of being invisible and unimportant continued into her adult life. Her first husband came out as gay. Her sister, Sophia, ended all contact with her, maybe because Olivia knew about dark family secrets in Sophia's life that she was trying to hide. Despite all of that, Olivia built a successful life. She was a loving, attentive mother whose children are thriving adults raising children of their own. She was a businesswoman who was integrally involved with her husband in the businesses they had built. Things seemed to be going fine, and then her first panic attack occurred while driving on the way to move closer to her mother. It made sense given her childhood experiences. She believed that driving was not fun, driving was unsafe, and driving meant she was alone. Olivia was moving closer to her mother, who she had experienced as mean and not safe to be around. She grew up feeling unimportant and invisible, and then her husband withdrew and began to treat her as insignificant and invisible. The combination of his treatment and the drive to see her mother caused her amygdala to sound an alarm, childhood monsters came out of the bottom drawer, and her anxiety came roaring back.

Olivia worked fearlessly with EMDR therapy and improved immensely. She uncovered the connections between her childhood experiences, her core beliefs, and her anxiety. She remembered that she had a passion for the less fortunate and found a way to help them. She was able to accept that the changes in her husband's personality and his treatment of her were not his choices, but a consequence of his medical condition and treatment. She did what her husband suggested she do; she built a life for herself.

Other consequences of trauma mentioned in Chapter 1 included Trauma Glasses and Magnet Moments. Like moving out of the cortex and into the limbic system or brainstem, or like monsters coming out of the bottom drawer, it is easy to look at the world through Trauma Glasses or focus on Magnet Moments without ever knowing what we are doing.

8

TRAUMA GLASSES

> *"Unlike simple stress, trauma changes your view of your life and yourself. It shatters your most basic assumptions about yourself and your world"*
> – MARK GOULSTON

*I*magine putting on a pair of glasses by lifting your hands to either side of your face (whether you wear glasses or not). Imagine the color of the frames, how thin or thick the frames are – how do they look? Are they stylish or outdated? Suppose that these imagined frames are so large that they cover your entire visual field; you can only see things through these lenses. When putting on a pair of glasses, there is always a moment of adjustment after putting them on – the brain is readjusting to see what is in front and the side of you through the lenses. If the lenses are clean and clear, you can see things clearly and in focus.

Now, *imagine putting* on a different pair of glasses (yes, lift your hands to the sides of your head again!) that have lenses covered with smudges, fingerprints, and debris. Close your eyes for a moment and imagine those glasses with the dirty lenses. Imagine what you see now. Is it difficult to see anything in front of you, or to the side of you, with any clarity? How do you feel when you try to look at what is in front of you, and you cannot see things? Do you feel frustrated, annoyed, irritated, or sad? You try to clean the lenses, but the smudges, fingerprints, and debris are embedded in the lenses. So, you experience every place you go, everything you see, and every person you encounter through these dirty lenses or obstructions. You probably know where we are going with this. The obstructions on the lenses are the memories of the distressing events that you have experienced in your life; the ones you remember (explicit memories) and the ones you don't (implicit memories). So, when you look in front of you, to either side or even backward, you see everything through the filter of your memories. (See **Image A** on page 93 for more about explicit and implicit memories).

The memory of any distressing event is actually our perception of the event, not the factual truth of the event. So, in times of distress, we store information about those events in fragments. This contributes to those events being distorted in our memory. We recall events based on what we were seeing, hearing, tasting, touching, or smelling at the time of the event. Recalling memories alters the original memory, so the memory is constructed and reconstructed, shuffled and reshuffled, added to and subtracted from based on later experiences. All this restructuring of memories contributes to the smudges, fingerprints, and debris on the trauma lenses of our lives.

Let's look at the example of Lisa*. She lived in the Midwest with her depressed, alcoholic parents, and three siblings, one older and two younger. Lisa was a small child who looked much younger than her age. She was the target of all her mother's anger, resentments, and depression. The abuse started when Lisa was three years old and lasted until she was nine years old. The physical abuse was severe with beatings multiple times a week, sometimes daily. There was horrendous ritualistic torment. Her mother would force her to lay face down, flat on her bed with an object on her back. If Lisa shifted, the object would fall to the wood floor. Her mother would hear the object fall and come in to beat her because she moved. Her mother would also force her to squat against the wall for long periods of time. If Lisa moved, she would be berated and beaten. Her mother would withhold food saying that it cost too much to feed Lisa but would feed her siblings in front of her.

One day Lisa was in her bedroom on the top bunk, and her mother yanked her arm so hard that Lisa fell to the ground. She gashed her head open, blood gushed everywhere, and her arm was broken. Her mother dragged her by her other arm to the bathroom sink, so that Lisa would bleed in the sink instead of making a mess on the floor. When her father came in to see what happened, her mother lied, saying she fell. Her father walked away without showing any concern for her. Lisa's mother did not take her to the doctor for days. When she did, the doctor noticed many bruises on her in various stages of healing but did not ask any questions about how she got them. The pattern of Lisa's life was daily abuse of one form or another.

Sexual abuse by her father started when she was five years old and continued until she was nine and her parents died in a car crash. Having never been to therapy in her life, Lisa came to see me when she was 34-years old. Although she was single, she wanted to be married and have children, but the memory monsters in her state-level drawer were too much for her to handle. She had a lot of anger, rage, and trouble with relationships in all areas – work, friendships, and intimates. Her lenses had smudges of both physical and sexual abuse, fingerprints of adults not taking care of her, especially physicians and teachers, and core belief debris that she had no value, was worthless, unlovable, and was only suited to be used and abused by others.

In short, she had a distorted view of life. Her parents, who were biologically engineered to love her, severely abused her. Teachers did not seem to notice that she came to school disheveled with uncombed hair, a dirty body, and in dirty clothes. Physicians did not inquire further about the abrasions and bruises on her body, that she was underweight, and appeared to be a child who was failing to thrive. As a result, Lisa could only see her life through the trauma glasses of an abused child.

Lisa's counseling focused on healing her traumatic memories by using a combination of EMDR Therapy, Relationship Therapy, and Reality Therapy. It took a while to clean the smudges off her trauma glasses because Lisa was programmed to believe that she was terrible and deserved all the abuse that she had gotten. If she had *been better*, they would not have hurt her; if she had value, the teachers and doctors would have helped her, so it must be that she was bad and valueless. Changing the fingerprints of her memories took effort and time on her part, but slowly she was able to see herself for who she really was – a small child who deserved to be treated well, cared for, and loved. She began to understand that she was not to blame. Her parents, as adults, were the only ones responsible. She was only a small child. She could not be responsible for how they treated her, nor for the failure of the other adults in her life. She was supposed to be protected but wasn't. The debris on her glasses was made up of her beliefs and perceptions of those traumatic events. She stored those beliefs from an abused child's perspective. When looking at those memories from an adult's view, she knew that she was not to blame. Lisa was able to destroy the trauma glasses she had worn since she was a child, and finally realized she did not need glasses at all.

9

MAGNET MOMENTS

> *"No one ever told me how sorrow traumatizes your heart, making you think it will never beat exactly the same way again"*
>
> — SARAH NOFFKE

If I asked you to think about the story, or stories, of your life, which stories would you remember? What experiences would you focus on to tell your story? Would the memories be the ones that made you feel excited and alive? Or would your moments be about events that hurt you, made you sad, angry, or depressed? Would these memory moments tell a fairy tale, a comedy, or a tragedy? What becomes the focus of our memories is based on how we perceived the experiences, whether those experiences were positive or negative, how the memories were stored in the brain, and the fact that memories change each time we think about them. I call these *magnet moments,* the ones that stick to the surface, and seem to be the quickest to retrieve when sharing our story. How many of you have magnets on your refrigerator? I have many. I collect magnets from every place I go in my travels. So, when I see these magnets, they remind me of the travel adventures I have had.

Now, imagine your refrigerator is covered with magnets from the distressing events in your life. Imagine going to the refrigerator to get some blueberries, and you see the magnet of a woman in the ER with a black and blue eye because her husband punched her. Imagine wanting strawberries from the refrigerator only to see the magnet of that same woman with a bloody nose. Imagine a magnet with a picture of a sexually abused child, or the magnet of your lying, cheating husband. How would you feel when you looked at your refrigerator with these magnets and the stories they told? And, why would you want to put those tragic reminders on your refrigerator anyway?

Well, the refrigerator represents your body-mind system and the magnet moments are the scars, or triggers, those unprocessed events left in the state-level drawer of your brain. When these memories are not processed or integrated, it is like sticking those tragic magnets on your refrigerator to keep distressing, or triggering, you every time you go to the refrigerator.

These magnet moments are stuck to us and impact our daily functioning by starting negative memory loops that play over and over. How many of you have replayed an event, or a regret, over and over in your mind, possibly for years? These are your magnet moments. Sometimes the actual memory may be hidden, but the feelings associated with the memory are ever-present. These feelings cause a chemical reaction in the gut that sends a signal to the brain to think about things that make you feel the way you did when the event happened. This chemical reaction sends a signal back to the gut to "feel" more of that feeling, and so on, and so on until the loop of negative moments is dictating how you feel, think, act, and behave.[39]

One of my magnet moments started when I was nine years old. A family member and an older neighborhood boy abused me from the age of nine to 11-years old. I absolutely loved softball when I was a kid, and then my softball coach said he wanted to have sex with me. The rest of my adolescence and early adult life was "magneted" by these memories. The façade that I presented was that everything was okay with me, but inside I was a churning volcano of anger. The volcano was churning all the time, so it did not take much to make me blow. I was stirred up all the time. I would get triggered; my state-level drawer would open, I would blow-up by screaming and yelling, and then it would take weeks after the blow-up for me to figure out why I was so angry. The feeling I got after the blow up was terrible. I hated yelling. Hated it. I hated being yelled at as a kid, but I did not think I could not stop myself as an adult. It was a double whammy; the behavior was modeled to me as a child, and the abuse created magnet moment triggers. I tried to stop, really tried, and I would beat myself up with all the negative core beliefs of "something is wrong with me; I am a horrible person; I am worthless", and so on. I would make a commitment never to yell again, and then I would get triggered, and the volcano would blow. It was an ugly, vicious cycle.

Another magnet moment came from my abusive marriage. My story goes like many– met a guy in college, fell in love (not sure what that even means), dated two years, got married, quit school, had two children, went back to school to finish the first degree, and got divorced. Total time from dating to divorce was 21 years. Those years were probably typical of people who get married when they are young with an enchanted understanding of love and marriage. But what about the dysregulation (the volcano!!!), unresolved trauma, and unresolved emotions that were brought into and were part of the marriage? Remember, trauma is anything that is prolonged, overwhelming, or unpredictable.[40] People change, life changes; things change.

I had suspicions that something had changed with him. I noticed things between him and his married secretary, things that did not seem "right." So, one day I asked my husband if he was having an affair. With stone-cold eyes and no emotion in his voice, he responded, "You are not nice, I don't love you anymore." I was taken aback, stunned. Wait, what? I was numb, it was like being hit with ice-cold water and not having any feeling. The only thought I had was, "Nice deflection dude, but answer the question!" He never answered the question, but this seemed to spark the nightmare of the next year. I was finishing the last year of my bachelor's degree, taking 18 hours a semester, working a 20-hour a week job, and raising two children. I was in complete survival mode. I shut down my emotions to survive and tried to figure out what was happening. I had to keep my thoughts focused: "I can do one more day, I can make it through one more day." I knew what I was thinking about and focused on, but I had no idea what he was thinking, other than I knew his focus was on his secretary. I know what I experienced in that last year– extreme torment, verbal abuse, emotional manipulation, and discovering that he had been having the affair for four years with her. I discovered he had been having other affairs for 15 years of the marriage.

Next came physical beatings. There were five total beatings; the last one landed me in the emergency room, and the police escorted my husband from the house. He was begging me not to press charges, or have the police take him. He said, "Do you want me to go to jail?" I was standing before him with the police waiting for my response. I could feel the lump rising on my back where he had been pummeling me just minutes before. I could feel the knot in my head throbbing where he repeatedly pounded my head against the solid wood door. I could see the soccer ball sized clump of hair ripped from my head. I could feel my entire body aching. I was in disbelief. All I could respond with was, "I wanted you to stop beating me." Two weeks later I moved out. These are the magnet moments of that marriage. The magnets I kept on my refrigerator for a while, until I found the right therapy that healed my state-level drawer and destroyed those magnets.

When people look at me, they probably see someone who is educated and confident. These are both true, but what people do not see are the magnet moments, or scars. Not scars on my body, but in my body. Sure, I have physical scars on my body; one on my shin from falling on a rusty nail when I was a kid, a scar on my right pointer finger where I gouged an inch of skin out, and a dent in my nose where my husband hit me. I have scars from multiple surgeries – some elective (foot surgery), others not elective (cancer). The scars that people do not see are the scars inside me – the magnet moment scars. Scars so deep even a body scan does not show them. The scars of childhood abuse, my emotionally and physically absent father who died when I was 13-years-old, being married to an abusive, lying, cheating man, and the emotional scars of core beliefs that I was inferior, worthless, unlovable, and rejected. These were the magnet moments that created the story of my life. Every time I looked at my 'refrigerator', I saw magnets that confirmed that I was inferior to others, so I had to work ten times as hard just to feel somewhat equal. I saw magnets that made me feel worthless, so I had to find ways to prove I had worth by getting an education (with the student loans to prove it!!). I saw magnets that said I was unlovable because of the abuse by multiple people; and the confirmation that others rejected me. I did a good job hiding my magnets, or at least I tried. These magnet moments would not stay hidden though, they came out of my state-level drawer as angry behaviors when I became triggered and perceived danger, even when there was no real, present danger.

The magnet moments told my life story of all the abuse, so I had difficulty seeing the other parts of my life that were good, positive, and rewarding. I went to counseling... lots of counseling! I was sick of hearing my own story, ad nauseam sick (finger in mouth, throwing up sick), because we kept moving and I would have to find a new counselor. I finally found a therapy that got to the state-level drawer, healed the triggers in that drawer, destroyed the volcano, healed my emotions, and healed the story of my life. So, now my magnet moments look wholly different and tell an entirely different story. My story now is one of being grateful for my life, grateful for having a great group of friends, and grateful for the blessings in my personal and professional life.

10

HOW TO KNOW

> *"Remembering the sensations is how we remember memories"*
> —BESSEL VAN DER KOLK

We all cope with bad experiences in a variety of ways, some healthy, some less than healthy, and some that are self-destructive. Healthy coping includes talking with friends, positive activities like exercise, yoga, massage, pedicures, laughing, cleaning out the junk closets, cooking, gardening, or other outdoor activities. Less healthy ways of coping, but not necessarily self-destructive (if kept in moderation) ways, might include eating, drinking, binge watching shows, shopping, or sleeping. Shopping is sometimes known as "retail therapy", and Friday Happy Hour after a stressful week of work is almost a national tradition. Some self-destructive attempts to cope with bad experiences include excessive drinking, drug use, smoking, excessive spending, excessive eating, self-harming behaviors, sleeping to escape, and/or temper tantrums. Adults do have temper tantrums; we just usually call them something else, like anger outbursts, rage episodes, or revenge.

At some point, people realize that "I should be over this by now" just isn't true

When these efforts to cope with the aftermath of trauma do not relieve the pain, fear, depression, anxiety, or anger, people sometimes seek therapy. Often, they seek therapy when life becomes unmanageable or someone else like an employer, a spouse, or a parent, requires or demands it. At some point, people begin to realize that the notion "I should be able to deal with this on my own" or "I should be over this by now" just isn't true. One of those people was Carrie. She came to therapy when her fear became unmanageable, when it began haunting her daily and made dealing with everyday experiences almost impossible. She was living in constant fear of being attacked, and she trusted no one. For her, coming to therapy took immense courage. Still, she began therapy with the hope that her fear could subside, and her life could get better.

Ellen started therapy when she realized her life was becoming unmanageable because she was beginning to zone out and lose time. Her episodes of zoning out were beginning to affect her work and she was tired of feeling unsafe. Lisa's pent up anger hampered her relationships so much she thought she would not be able to get married. Anger like this brings many people into therapy either because, like Lisa, it is interfering in their relationships, or they are just tired of feeling angry. Frequent or intense anger outbursts can make others dislike you, avoid you, damage relationships, cost you your job, and/or cause you to feel shame for things you have done.

Sadness over the loss of emotional closeness with her husband is what brought Olivia to therapy, combined with anxiety that interfered with her doing the things she wanted. She already had many good coping skills when she came, since she had been in therapy before. Therapy helped her immensely because she was unwilling to settle for just *some* improvement and she was willing to try something new, like EMDR. At the other extreme is another client, Shelly, who came to therapy because she was suicidal. She had reached the point that death almost seemed like the only way out, but she wasn't 100% there. She also was willing to trust her therapist and try something new and intense – EMDR. And Jules, who sought out therapy to heal memories because of a lack of attachment to her mother. She wanted to feel connected to others and knew she needed help to heal.

Not All Bad Experiences Take Years of Therapy

The clients we have talked about have spent considerable time in therapy working to heal and integrate their memories. But not everyone suffering from the results of bad experiences needs long-term therapy. Therapy is individual, personal, and a matter of degree. Not everyone who comes to therapy has had horrible childhoods either. Some people come to therapy to resolve a present-day issue. Many of the people who come to therapy grew up in stable, loving homes, and are successful people who had something distressing happen to them. Those events can be anything based on a person's personality, their core beliefs, who else was involved, and the overall impact of the event. The goal of therapy is to help people heal and integrate both big "T" and small "t" traumas, so that they can pursue their dreams and live the life they want.

Louis* came to therapy because he felt "emotionally muted." He was a successful professional with a family who loved and supported him. He recognized he wanted more self-confidence and a higher level of emotional satisfaction. Like many people, he brought a core belief of *"I'm not good enough"* with him from childhood, despite growing up in a family that loved and cared for him. EMDR therapy helped him release that self-limiting belief and increase his self-confidence, so that he could pursue his goals. He did not require long-term therapy.

Some people come to therapy because of unfortunate experiences, like stillbirths, infertility, or the loss of children. Emma* is one of these clients. Emma is Grace's older sister, and they have three older brothers. Their parents had careers that required extensive travel to Africa and Australia, so all five children traveled with their parents. A governess home-schooled the children. Each of the girls would say that they had an exciting life as they enjoyed all the adventures and the closeness of the immediate family. Both sisters believed their parents loved them, but their parents were often preoccupied with their careers, which left the girls to fend for themselves after their brothers left for university in the United States. The sisters decided to go to separate universities, in different states, so they maintained contact through texting and video chatting. Grace got engaged and married two years before Emma got married. The sisters decided that it was important for them to raise their families together, so they moved to the same city to be close.

Emma came to therapy first. She had been unsuccessful getting pregnant and wanted to see if there was an underlying emotional reason. During the intake, she was unable to identify any prolonged, overwhelming, or unpredictable event, but did identify some negative core beliefs she had. So, we used EMDR Therapy to reprocess her negative beliefs and then created what is called a future template. For Emma, this primarily meant seeing herself being successful in getting pregnant and maintaining the pregnancy through delivery.

We worked on each of her negative core beliefs in EMDR Therapy sessions by addressing the beliefs one at a time. She was able to identify the origin of the negative belief, heal what needed to be healed, and replace the negative belief with a positive self-belief. Then it was time to work on her wanting to be pregnant. In starting the future template work, she was able to realize that she had a belief from childhood that she would never have kids. She remembered not liking having four other kids in the house to share her parents' time and attention. She had made a vow as a young child that she would never have kids. We had to remove this vow and replace it with the positive imagery that having kids was something she did want and desire. After clearing that vow, she was able to imagine herself getting pregnant and delivering a healthy baby. We took this future template slowly, imagining each month that the fetus was growing, month-by-month, until time for delivery. Then she was able to imagine a successful delivery. Emma also wanted to use EMDR to visualize being a good mom, loving and caring for her baby, and her baby growing up healthy, happy, and strong. Four months after ending EMDR therapy with Emma, she sent an email to let me know she was eight weeks pregnant. Emma said that after doing EMDR therapy, she would sit quietly for a few minutes each day and re-visualize what she had visualized in therapy and was looking forward to having a healthy, happy baby.

11

WHO TO CHOOSE

"Trauma is personal. It does not disappear if it is not validated. When it is ignored or invalidated the silent screams continue internally heard only by the one held captive. When someone enters the pain and hears the screams healing can begin"
                                        –DANIELLE BERNOCK

Many therapeutic approaches work at a cognitive level, or with the first drawer of the memory file cabinet. Cognitive Behavioral Therapy (CBT) and Trauma-Focused Cognitive Behavioral Therapy (TF-CBT), well known evidence-based therapies that are practiced by numerous mental health professionals, are based on the premise that thoughts about an event lead to feelings about the event, and then thoughts and feelings together lead to behaviors. Sometimes it does work that way, but not always. For example, if you trip over a toy left in the middle of the floor and your thought is, "I should have been looking where I stepped," you might feel embarrassed or foolish, move the toy and go on. If your thought is "I told those kids to put their toys away, it is their fault I tripped," you may feel angry and punish the kids for leaving the toy out. The first reaction is a cognitive reaction and the second is an emotional reaction.

There are many kinds of therapy and a myriad of studies about what makes therapy work. Among the factors that make therapy successful are your expectations that it will help, and your relationship with the therapist. Since there are a multitude of different types of therapy and not all therapists offer all types of therapy, here are some steps to help you choose a therapist. Since you are reading this book, we assume you might need a trauma therapist. Research shows that EMDR, Somatic Experiencing, Neurofeedback, Yoga, Trauma-informed yoga, Internal Family Systems, and expressive therapies like art, drama, and music are the most powerfully effective modalities in healing trauma.

Most people choose a therapist by asking friends for a recommendation, checking their insurance company's provider directory, or searching online. Those are reasonable ways to start. When you have some names of potential therapists, look to see if the therapist has a website. The website should tell you what types of therapy the therapist offers and should have a short biographical description. *Psychology Today* has an online directory of therapists that can be searched by city, zip code, and by a specific type of therapy. There are associations for most of the different kinds of therapy, like the EMDR International Association (EMDRIA), that have online therapist directories to assist potential clients in finding the right therapist by city and state.

Another consideration is whether you want to go to an agency, a private group practice, or a sole practitioner. Many agencies can see people regardless of their ability to pay for services. Agencies have a variety of therapists and may provide other services in addition to therapy, like case management, coordination with other social services and access to an on-site psychiatrist. Private practice therapists, either in group practices or sole practitioner offices, may have more ability to focus on an area of therapy and often receive specialized training and certifications. They may also be able to offer a higher degree of privacy than an agency.

When you find a therapist, you think might be the right fit for you, call and ask questions. Ask whether the therapist can help with the issue, or issues, you have, what the office hours are, and how soon you could get an appointment. Pay attention to how you feel while talking to the therapist or the office staff. Therapists are responsible for how their staff treats potential clients. If it doesn't feel right, if you feel discounted, dismissed, or if you do not get a call back within a day, find a different therapist.

Understand that the first session or two with will be intake sessions. You will be filling out new client forms (unless they are available online) and the therapist will ask questions to gather relevant background information about you and the reason you are seeking therapy. During the intake process, it is important to feel heard and to feel that the therapist has a genuine interest in helping you. It is essential to pay attention to your instincts and feelings, and at the same time, keep in mind that it can take some time to build rapport and trust. You should feel free to ask questions about the therapist's experience, training, thoughts about whether he or she can help you, and how long therapy might take. The therapist's responsibility is to guide you toward healing and help you change your life in a way that makes it more satisfying and enjoyable to you. Therapy is for you and about you.

Therapy is for you and about you

12

RECAP!

"All healing is first a healing of the heart"
−CARL TOWNSEND

This book is intended to provide information about trauma, how it affects you, and how to begin the healing process. We used real case examples to show the different traumatic experiences some of our clients have had, and how they were able to heal and integrate the memories of the past. In healing the memories, they were able to decide how to live the rest of their lives free from the past. We hope you now have some knowledge of the process and will be inspired to do the work necessary to heal your traumatic, or distressing, memories. The process of trauma therapy will differ for each person, even if two individuals experienced the same traumatic event. This difference is due to our temperament, personality, and how the brain processes information. We believe it is possible to heal from trauma and integrate the memories back into the whole of a person, so that the experiences no longer negatively impact his or her life. We hope we have removed the stigma that going to therapy means that something is wrong with you, or you are defective. What we hope is that you will seek therapeutic help to heal your emotional wounds, *because we all have wounds.*

We are grateful to the neuroscientists, trauma researchers, play therapists, clinicians, and clients who have provided a wealth of knowledge, so that we can be successful with trauma work. We measure success by the improvement our clients make, and it is a joy to watch the transformation of clients from the beginning of therapy to the end. There is an abundance of literature available for further study of the neurobiology of trauma and healing. Some of our favorite authors include, but are not limited to, Dr. Bessel van der Kolk, Dr. Bruce Perry, Dr. Daniel Siegel, Dr. Peter Levine, Dr. Joseph LeDoux, Dr. Eliana Gil, Dr. Garry Landreth, Dr. Kevin O'Connor, Dr. Charles Schaefer, Dr. Robin Shapiro, Dr. Ann Jernberg and Phyllis Booth, Dr. Terry Kottman, Dr. William Steele, and Dr. Virginia Axline.

APPENDIX

"Healing is a matter of time, but it is sometimes also a matter of opportunity"

HIPPOCRATES

TREATMENT OPTIONS

Below is a brief overview of common therapeutic treatment approaches for trauma. The descriptions are taken ***directly*** from the websites of the different approaches and are intended to provide a short introduction to the approach to help you choose the option that will work best for you. The website address is provided for each approach, so the reader can research further information about the different approaches. It is important to choose a therapeutic approach that will get to the core of the issue where the state-level memory is activated for the most effective reprocessing and healing. Doing a Google search will identify other therapeutic treatment methods, but we believe the following methods are the best to heal trauma memories:

Eye Movement Desensitization and Reprocessing Therapy (EMDR) (www.emdria.org/)

Eye Movement Desensitization and Reprocessing (EMDR) therapy is an integrative psychotherapy approach that has been extensively researched and proven effective for the treatment of trauma. EMDR is a set of standardized protocols that incorporates elements from many different treatment approaches. Dr. Francine Shapiro, in 1987, made an unintentional discovery that the intensity of disturbing thoughts could be reduced with eye movement. Through her research she was able to report in 1989 in the *Journal of Traumatic Stress,* the successful treatment of individuals who had been traumatized. EMDR Therapy has continued to develop and advance in the treatment of a variety of conditions as more and more therapists worldwide use this effective treatment protocol (www.emdria.org).

EMDR was originally established as a treatment protocol for post-traumatic stress, but clinicians report using the treatment for a variety of conditions. Here is a brief list of conditions that EMDR has effectively treated: Abuse, Addiction, Anxiety, Body Dysmorphic Disorder, Depression, Dissociative Disorders, Disturbing Memories, Future Success Imagery, Grief, Stress Reduction, Panic Attacks, and Performance/Performance Anxiety.

EMDR therapy is based on the Adaptive Information Processing Model. The model's basic assumption is that memory networks are the basis of clinical symptoms and mental health. The information processing system in our brains is geared for health. Given the right support our brains will move toward positive/adaptive resolution of distressing experiences. One of the goals of trauma therapy is to truly put these experiences in the past.

Neurofeedback (https://braincoretherapy.com/find-a-provider/)

Neurofeedback, also called EEG Biofeedback is a state-of-the-art, non-invasive, drugless method for teaching the brain to function in a more balanced and healthful way. A simple and pleasant learning modality that can help shift the way the brain produces and distributes its electrical energy. Four divisions of electrical impulses made by our brain, Delta, Theta, Alpha and Beta are called "Frequency Bands". These Frequency Bands tell us which parts of your brain are active and which frequency bands the brain should be using to complete a given task, activity or should be most active during different states of mind.

Individuals are connected to a computer using wires and sensors, thereby allowing the BrainCore technology to monitor the brainwave activity. The software automatically detects when the brainwaves are properly ordered and feeds that information back to the patient in real time. The feedback appears in the form of a game, movie, or sound which signals to the patient that the brainwaves are becoming more ordered. The patient's own brainwaves control the game, movie, or sound activity, and the observation of this dynamic helps the brain lean how to improve its own regulation (https://braincoretherapy.com/find-a-provider/).

Somatic Experiencing (SE) (www.traumahealing.org)

The Somatic Experiencing® method is a body-oriented approach to the healing of trauma and other stress disorders. It is the life's work of Dr. Peter A. Levine, resulting from his multidisciplinary study of stress physiology, psychology, ethology, biology, neuroscience, indigenous healing practices, and medical biophysics, together with over 45 years of successful clinical application. The SE approach releases traumatic shock, which is key to transforming PTSD and the wounds of emotional and early developmental attachment trauma. The SE Approach offers a framework to assess where a person is "stuck" in the fight, flight or freeze responses and provides clinical tools to resolve these fixated physiological states. It provides effective skills appropriate to a variety of healing professions including mental health, medicine, physical and occupational therapies, bodywork, addiction treatment, first response, education, and others. Like other somatic psychology approaches, Somatic Experiencing® professes a *body first* approach to dealing with the problematic (and, oftentimes, physical) symptoms of trauma. This means that therapy isn't about reclaiming memories or changing our thoughts and beliefs about how we feel but looking at the sensations that lie underneath our feelings and uncovering our habitual behavior patterns to these feelings (traumahealing.org).

Accelerated Experiential-Dynamic Psychotherapy (AEDP) (www.AEDPinstitute.org)

Developed by Dr. Diana Fosha, the author of the <u>The Transforming Power of Affect</u>, AEDP (Accelerated Experiential Dynamic Psychotherapy) is an ever-emergent model, ever-growing through the ongoing contributions of the AEDP faculty and the members of the AEDP community.

Crisis and suffering provide opportunities to awaken extraordinary capacities that otherwise might lie dormant, unknown, and untapped. AEDP is about experientially making the most of these opportunities for both healing and transformation.

Key to its therapeutic action is the undoing of aloneness and thus, the establishment of the therapeutic relationship experienced as both safe haven, and secure base. Once that's established, we work with emotional experience, working experientially toward healing trauma and suffering, and toward expanding emergent positive transformational experiences.

AEDP seeks to clinically make neuroplasticity happen. Championing our innate healing capacities, AEDP has roots in and resonances with many disciplines — among them interpersonal neurobiology, attachment theory, emotion theory and affective neuroscience, body-focused approaches, and finally, transformational studies.

Through undoing of aloneness, and through the in-depth processing of difficult emotional and relational experiences, as well as new transformational experiences, the AEDP clinician fosters the emergence of new and healing experiences for the client, and with them resources, resilience and a renewed zest for life (www.AEDPinstitute.org).

Somatic Transformation (www.Somatic-Transformation.org)

Somatic Transformation is a healing modality that uses relational and bodily-centered practices to help people change the imprint of trauma. Whether in the form of early emotional neglect or overwhelming adverse events, trauma alienates people from others, themselves, even their own bodies, generating a profound sense of loneliness and separation from humanity.

Inspired by neuroscience, developmental psychology, and somatic healing practices from traditional societies, Somatic Transformation seeks to identify and then integrate an individual's bodily-based, intuitive wisdom with the abstract knowledge of the mind through six therapeutic practices: Somatic Empathy,

Embodiment, Somatic Awareness, Somatic Inquiry, Somatic Intervention, and Somatic Reflection. The term somatic comes from the Greek word soma, which refers to unity between the body and mind.

Trauma disrupts healthy functioning of the brain and nervous system, creating dysregulated neural states that negatively affect personality, physical and mental health, and behavior. Somatic Interventions are exercises and meditations designed to regulate the chronic neural patterns of hyperarousal, hypoarousal, anxiety, and depression. When we can identify and shift dysregulated neural states in the moment through somatic practices, we can teach the disturbed autonomic nervous system to maintain more optimal states for growth and development.

Another function of Somatic Interventions is to restore higher cortical processing, often interrupted in moments of trauma. Embodiment of sensory-based images, dreams, and archetypes can awaken vitality, guide the full re-consolidation of anguishing memories, and restore organization and meaning to a person's inner world. These Somatic Interventions can make use of music, drama, and creative writing, but are most often centered around drawings that represent sensory experience, allowing the subcortical elements of trauma to be reconnected with more complex cortical processing (www.Somatic-Transformation.org).

Internal Family Systems (https://selfleadership.org/about-internal-family-systems.html)

The IFS Model, which evolved as a result of this exploration, views a person as containing an ecology of relatively discrete minds, each of which has valuable qualities and each of which is designed to -- and wants to -- play a valuable role within. These parts are forced out of their valuable roles, however, by life experiences that can reorganize the system in unhealthy ways. A good analogy is an alcoholic family in which the children are forced into protective and stereotypic roles by the extreme dynamics of their family. While one finds similar sibling roles across alcoholic families (e.g., the scapegoat, mascot, lost child), one does not conclude that those roles represent the essence of those children. Instead, each child is unique and, once released from his or her role by intervention, can find interests and talents separate from the demands of the chaotic family. The same process seems to hold true for internal families -- parts are forced into extreme roles by external circumstances and, once it seems safe, they gladly transform into valuable family members.

What circumstances force these parts into extreme and sometimes destructive roles? Trauma is one factor, and the effects of childhood sexual abuse on internal families has been discussed at length (Goulding and Schwartz, 1995). But more often, it is a person's family of origin values and interaction patterns that create internal polarizations which escalate over time and are played out in other relationships. This, also, is not a novel observation; indeed, it is a central tenet of object relations and self-psychology. What is novel to IFS is the attempt to understand all levels of human organization -- intrapsychic, family, and culture -- with the same systemic principles, and to intervene at each level with the same ecological techniques (https://selfleadership.org/about-internal-family-systems.html).

Organic Intelligence & Trauma
(www.OrganicIntelligence.org)

Organic Intelligence® (**OI**) is a unique theory and clinical practice of human empowerment, resiliency, and compassion to resolve the devastating effects of stress, trauma, and PTSD. The Organic Intelligence (OI) clinical protocol suggests that, from a systems perspective, what's wrong with therapy *is the focus on what's wrong* — including the focus on trauma.

Organic Intelligence brings a necessary shift in perspective from pathology and trauma to the proven methods drawn from the wisdom of mindfulness and the science of self-organization. OI teaches how healing happens from the nervous system up and makes it possible to imagine freedom from suffering. Freedom from suffering becomes freedom for living an authentic, vibrant life in the here-and-now.

OI teaches therapists how to observe relevant client behaviors according to a very clear map. This mapping allows therapists to understand the nervous system state and reveals what kind of intervention is most likely to support natural systemic reorganization.

Rather than providing insight per se, Organic Intelligence aims to shepherd observable physio-emotional states according to a protocol which aligns with subtle, but naturally occurring organismic trends toward increased coherence — the rhythm of an integrative biology. We employ a 'shaping' paradigm of positive reinforcement — a true paradigm shift in trauma therapy. Organic Intelligence was developed by Steve Hoskinson, MA, MAT, who has trained thousands of practitioners and mentored trauma resolution instructors in North America, Europe, the Middle East, and Asia (www.OrganicIntelligence.org).

Creative Arts (www.nccata.org)

Creative Arts Therapists (CAT) are mental health professionals who use distinct arts-based methods and creative processes for the purpose of improving mental health wellness, physical illness, and disability. Under the CAT Association are six distinct creative therapies that include: Art Therapy, Dance Therapy, Music Therapy, Group Psychotherapy and Psychodrama, Drama Therapy, and Poetry Therapy. Each of these six therapies has an association specific to the type of therapeutic approach that will be identified below. Each of these different creative arts therapy has a desired outcome for overall mental, physical, and emotional health improvement, which include improving social, cognitive, and cognitive functioning, learning to better express self and needs through communication The National Coalition of Creative Arts Therapies Associations, Inc. (NCCATA), founded in 1979, is an alliance of membership associations dedicated to the advancement of the creative arts therapies professions. NCCATA is a coalition with membership organizations that represents over 15,000 individual members of six creative arts therapies associations nationwide (www.nccata.org).

Art Therapy (http://www.arttherapy.org/)

Art therapy emerged in the 1940s as a mental health profession in which clients, facilitated by the art therapist, use art media, the creative process, and the resulting artwork to explore their feelings, reconcile emotional conflicts, foster self- awareness, manage behavior and addictions, develop social skills, improve reality orientation, reduce anxiety, and increase self-esteem. A master's degree is required for entry-level practice in art therapy (http://www.arttherapy.org/).

Dance Therapy (http://www.adta.org)

Based on the empirically supported premise that the body, mind, and spirit are interconnected, dance/movement therapy is the psychotherapeutic use of movement to further the emotional, cognitive, physical, and social integration of the individual. Dance/movement therapy is practiced in mental health, rehabilitation, medical, educational, and forensic settings, and in nursing homes, day care centers, disease prevention, private practice, and health promotion programs. Training and education occur on the graduate level (http://www.adta.org).

Music Therapy (http://www.musictherapy.org/)

Founded in 1950, AMTA defines music therapy as the clinical and evidence-based use of music interventions to accomplish individualized goals within a therapeutic relationship by a credentialed professional who has completed an approved music therapy program. Music therapists structure the use of both instrumental and vocal music strategies to facilitate changes that are non-musical in nature. Music therapists assess emotional well-being, physical health, social functioning, communication abilities, and cognitive skills through musical responses. They design music sessions for individuals and groups based on client needs using a variety of techniques and approaches. Research shows that music therapy facilitates numerous clinical outcomes in areas such as: rehabilitation; habilitation; social, emotional, and cognitive functioning; and learning (http://www.musictherapy.org/).

Group Psychotherapy and Psychodrama (http://www.asgpp.org)

The ASGPP promotes the development of creativity, spontaneity and encounter to enhance the relationship between individuals, families and communities, and works actively to heal and transform society through the knowledge and practice of psychodrama, group psychotherapy and sociometry in all its diverse applications (http://www.asgpp.org).

Drama Therapy (http://www.nadta.org)

Drama Therapy has been an established health profession since 1979. In Drama Therapy, theatre-based processes are used within a therapeutic relationship to address physical, emotional, cognitive, and social needs of individuals, couples, families, and groups. After assessing the strengths and needs of clients, qualified drama therapists provide the indicated treatment including improvising scenes, role-playing challenging situations, or creating performances to raise awareness, change attitudes, and rehearse possible solutions to issues of concern (http://www.nadta.org).

Poetry Therapy (http://www.poetrytherapy.org)

For more than 30 years, NAPT members have forged a community of healers and lovers of words and language. We are psychotherapists, counselors, psychologists, social workers, and psychiatrists. We work in many settings where people deal with personal and communal pain and the search for growth. As poetry therapists, we use all forms of literature and the language arts, and we are united by our love of words, and our passion for enhancing the lives of others and ourselves (http://www.poetrytherapy.org).

Trauma Yoga (http://nrepp.samhsa.gov/)

Yoga has been studied through a grant by the National Institutes of Health as a viable treatment option for individuals with trauma. Trauma Center Trauma-Sensitive Yoga (TCTSY) is an empirically validated, adjunctive clinical treatment for complex trauma or chronic, treatment-resistant PTSD. Developed at the Trauma Center in Brookline, Massachusetts, TCTSY has foundations in Trauma Theory, Attachment Theory, and Neuroscience as well as deep roots in Yoga. TC-TSY aims to support emotion regulation, stabilization, and skill building for adults with chronic, treatment-resistant posttraumatic stress disorder (PTSD); complex PTSD; dissociative disorders; and other related emotional and behavioral problems.

The program is based on the central components of the hatha style of yoga, which focuses on integrating breathing and meditation with a set of physical postures and movements. In TC-TSY, elements of traditional hatha yoga are modified to maximize tolerance, build trauma survivors' experiences of empowerment, and cultivate a more positive relationship to one's body. Trauma-informed alterations to accommodate unique needs and sensitivities include prioritizing gentleness in movement, removing strongly suggestive language, de-emphasizing posture intensity, eliminating hands-on assistance from the instructor, and highlighting opportunities for participants to adjust the practice and make selections that feel appropriate for themselves. The four overarching themes of the intervention are to 1) experience the present moment, 2) make choices, 3) take effective action, and 4) create rhythms (http://nrepp.samhsa.gov/).

Play Therapy – Sand Tray Therapy (www.a4pt.org/)

The Association for Play Therapy (APT) is a national professional society established in 1982 to foster contact among mental health professionals interested in exploring and, when developmentally appropriate, applying the therapeutic power of play to communicate with and treat clients, particularly children. APT defines play therapy as "the systematic use of a theoretical model to establish an interpersonal process wherein trained play therapists use the therapeutic powers of play to help clients prevent or resolve psychosocial difficulties and achieve optimal growth and development. "Research suggests Play Therapy is an effective mental health approach, regardless of age, gender, or the nature of the problem, and works best when a parent, family member, or caretaker is actively involved in the treatment process (www.a4pt.org).

More simply put, child play therapy is a way of being with the child that honors their unique developmental level and looks for ways of helping in the "language" of the child – play. Licensed mental health professionals therapeutically use play to help their clients, most often children ages three to 12 years, to better express themselves and resolve their problems.

Play Therapy works best when a safe relationship is created between the therapist and client, one in which the latter may freely and naturally express both what pleases and bothers them. Mental health agencies, schools, hospitals, and private practitioners have

utilized Play Therapy as a primary intervention or as supportive therapy for:
- Behavioral problems, such as anger management, grief and loss, divorce and abandonment, and crisis and trauma.
- Behavioral disorders, such as anxiety, depression, attention deficit hyperactivity (ADHD), autism or pervasive developmental, academic and social developmental, physical and learning disabilities, and conduct disorders (www.a4pt.org).

IMAGE A

How Trauma Impacts Four Different Types of Memory

EXPLICIT MEMORY		IMPLICIT MEMORY	
SEMANTIC MEMORY	**EPISODIC MEMORY**	**EMOTIONAL MEMORY**	**PROCEDURAL MEMORY**
What It Is The memory of general knowledge and facts.	**What It Is** The autobiographical memory of an event or experience – including the who, what, and where.	**What It Is** The memory of the emotions you felt during an experience.	**What It Is** The memory of how to perform a common task without actively thinking about it.
Example You remember what a bicycle is.	**Example** You remember who was there and what street you were on when you fell off your bicycle in front of a crowd.	**Example** When a wave of shame or anxiety grabs you the next time you see your bicycle after the big fall.	**Example** You can ride a bicycle automatically, without having to stop and recall how it's done.
How Trauma Can Affect It Trauma can prevent information (like words, images, sounds, etc.) from different parts of the brain from combining to make a semantic memory.	**How Trauma Can Affect It** Trauma can shutdown episodic memory and fragment the sequence of events.	**How Trauma Can Affect It** After trauma, a person may get triggered and experience painful emotions, often without context.	**How Trauma Can Affect It** Trauma can change patterns of procedural memory. For example, a person might tense up and unconsciously alter their posture, which could lead to pain or even numbness.
Related Brain Area The temporal lobe and inferior parietal cortex collect information from different brain areas to create semantic memory.	**Related Brain Area** The hippocampus is responsible for creating and recalling episodic memory.	**Related Brain Area** The amygdala plays a key role in supporting memory for emotionally charged experiences.	**Related Brain Area** The striatum is associated with producing procedural memory and creating new habits.

Temporal lobe — Inferior parietal lobe

Hippocampus

Amygdala

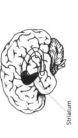

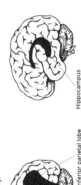

Striatum

nicabm
www.nicabm.com

© 2017 The National Institute for the Clinical Application of Behavioral Medicine

About the Authors

T. Susan Bachmann, MEd, LPC, NCC, EMDR Certified Therapist,
Amen Clinic Certified Brain Health Coach, Certified Emotion Code Practitioner, Certified Body Cody Code Practitioner
susan@ftrctulsa.org

Susan Bachmann is a Licensed Professional Counselor, a National Certified Counselor, a Certified Brain Health Coach through Amen Clinics and is a Certified therapist in Eye Movement

Desensitization and Reprocessing (EMDR), a certified Emotion Code Practitioner, and a certified Body Code Practitioner. Before becoming a therapist, she worked as a Certified Public Accountant in both public accounting and private industry. Because accounting felt confining and seemed to have limited positive human impact (she says accounting is about not making mistakes), she returned to school and earned a master's degree in counseling from the University of Houston. She began her career as a therapist working exclusively with traumatized children and their families and working to repair families disrupted by drug use, abuse, neglect, and foster care. Bachmann now focuses on helping adults and adolescents who have experienced traumatic events recover, set goals, and move forward. In addition, she often helps people work through the aftermath of stillbirths and grief. She is married, has two children, three grandchildren, and two dogs.

Kelly A. James, PhD, LPC, RPT-S, NCC, CCTP, CATP, CPC, EMDR Trained, Emotion Code Certified, Body Code Certified
info@drkellyajames.com

Kelly James received a doctorate from Regent University, School of Psychology and Counseling, two Master of Arts degrees from Oral Roberts University – Licensed Professional Counseling and Marriage and Family Therapy, and a Bachelor of Science in Psychology from the University of Arkansas. She is a Licensed Professional Counselor (LPC), Approved License Supervisor, National Board Certified Counselor (NCC), and Certified Clinical Trauma Professional, Child and Adolescent Trauma Professional (CATP), a Registered Play Therapist-Supervisor, Eye Movement Desensitization and Reprocessing (EMDR) Trained Therapist, Emotion Code Practitioner, and a Certified Professional Coach. She worked as an Employee Assistance Program (EAP) therapist and with children in traditional and therapeutic foster care for 10 years. Additionally, James has a private practice where she works with a variety of clientele including children, adolescents, and individual adults. James specializes in providing counseling to individuals who have experienced trauma, parenting skills training, and working with children with challenging behaviors. James has two children, James and Kaitlin, a daughter-in-law, Ashley, and two granddaughters, Cloey and Audrey.

ENDNOTES

[1] Adverse childhood experiences. (n.d.). Retrieved from https://www.samhsa.gov/capt/practicing-effective-prevention/prevention-behavioral-health/adverse-childhood-experiences

[2] Perry, B. D., & Szalavitz, M. (2017, p. 2). *The boy who was raised as a dog: And other stories from a child psychiatrist's notebook: What traumatized children can teach us about loss, love, and healing.* New York, NY: Basic Books.

[3] Search conducted on 08/06/2017

[4] Perry, B. D., & Szalavitz, M. (2017, p. 2).

[5] Trauma (n.d.). In *Cambridge advanced learner's dictionary & thesaurus online.* Retrieved from https://dictionary.cambridge.org/dictionary/english/trauma

[6] American Psychiatric Association. (2013). *Diagnostic and statistical manual of mental disorders* (5th ed.). Arlington, VA: American Psychiatric Publishing.

[7] Howard, S., & Crandall, M. W. (2007). Post traumatic stress disorder: What happens in the brain? *Washington Academy of Sciences,* 1-18. Retrieved from http://www.washacadsci.org/Journal/Journalarticles/V.93-3-Post%20Traumatic%20Stress%20Disorder.%20Sethanne%20Howard%20and%20Mark%20Crandalll.pdf

[8] Sharpiro, F. (2001, p. 7, 13). Eye Movement Desensitization and Reprocessing – Basic Principles, Protocols, and Procedures. New York: The Guilford Press.

[9] Perry, B., & Pollard, R. (1998, p. 36). Homeostasis, stress, trauma, and adaptation. A neurodevelopmental view of childhood trauma. *Child and Adolescent Psychiatric Clinics of North America, 7*(1), 33-51. Retrieved from http://psycnet.apa.org/record/1998-00036-003

[10] Perry, B. (2006, prologue p. 1). Applying principles of neurodevelopment to clinical work with maltreated and traumatized children: The neurosequential model of therapeutics. In N. Boyd Webb (Ed.), *Working with traumatized youth in child welfare* (pp. 27-52). New York, NY: The Guilford Press.

[11] Van der Kolk, B. (2015, p. 11). *The body keeps the score: Brain, mind, and body in the healing of trauma.* New York, NY: Penguin Books.

[12] Van der Kolk, B. (2015).

[13] Van der Kolk, B. (2015, p. 2).

[14] Perry, B. (2016, November, p. 5). The long shadow: Bruce Perry on the lingering effects of childhood trauma (J. Supin, Interviewer). *The Sun,* 4-13. Retrieved from https://childtrauma.org/wp-content/uploads/2016/12/Sun-interview-Bruce-Perry-Nov-2016.pdf

[15] Levine, P. (2015, p. xxi). *Trauma and memory: Brain and body in a search for the living past: A practical guide for understanding and working with traumatic memory.* Berkeley, CA: North Atlantic Books.

[16] Pert, C. (1997, p. 141). *Molecules of emotion.* New York, NY: Touchstone.

[17] Furness, H. (2017, April 19). Prince Harry: I sought counselling after 20 years of not thinking about the death of my mother, Diana, and two years of total chaos in my life. Retrieved from

http://www.telegraph.co.uk/news/2017/04/16/prince-harry-sought-counselling-death-mother-led-two-years-total/

[18] Furness, H. (2017, para. 2).

[19] Furness, H. (2017, para. 10-11).

[20] Ward, M. (2016, November 26). 5 things you didn't know about Prince Harry. *Vogue.* Retrieved from https://www.vogue.com/article/prince-harry-5-things-you-didn't-know

[21] Freud, S., & Hall, G. S. (2016). *A general introduction to psychoanalysis.* North Charleston, SC: CreateSpace.

[22] Perry, B. (2003). Keynote address. *Eye Movement Desensitization and Reprocessing International Association Conference.* San Diego, CA.

[23] Perry, B. (2003). Keynote address. *Eye Movement Desensitization and Reprocessing International Association Conference.* San Diego, CA.

[24] Perry, B. D., & Szalavitz, M. (2017). *The boy who was raised as a dog: And other stories from a child psychiatrist's notebook: What traumatized children can teach us about loss, love, and healing.* New York, NY: Basic Books.

[25] Sharpiro, F. (2001).

[26] Perry, B. (2003).

[27] Sorkin, A. (Producer). (1999). *The West Wing.* New York, NY: NBC.

[28] Steele, W. (2003). Helping traumatized children. In S. L. A. Strausner & N. K. Philips (Ed.), *Understanding mass violences: A social work*

perspective. (pp 41-56). New York: Allen and Bacon.

[29] Perry, B. D., & Szalavitz, M. (2017). *The boy who was raised as a dog: And other stories from a child psychiatrist's notebook: What traumatized children can teach us about loss, love, and healing.* New York, NY: Basic Books.

[30] Sukel, K. (January 26, 2015). Martha Farah. Retrieved from http://www.dana.org/News/Early_Life_Experience,_Critical_Periods,_and_Brain_Development

[31] Pert, C. (1997). *Molecules of emotion.* New York, NY: Touchstone.

[32] Perry, B. (2006). Applying principles of neurodevelopment to clinical work with maltreated and traumatized children: The neurosequential model of therapeutics. In N. Boyd Webb (Ed.), *Working with traumatized youth in child welfare* (pp. 27-52). New York, NY: The Guilford Press.

[33] Perry, B. (2006).

[34] Van der Kolk, B. (2015, p. 56). *The body keeps the score: Brain, mind, and body in the healing of trauma.* New York, NY: Penguin Books.

[35] Van der Kolk, B. (2015, p. 54).

[36] Perry, B. (2006).

[37] Perry, B. (2006).

[38] Aamodt, S., & Wang, S. (2012). *Welcome to your child's brain: How the mind grows from conception to college.* New York, NY: Bloomsbury.

[39] Dispenza, J. (2012). *Breaking the habit of being yourself: How to lose your*

mind and create a new one. Carlsbad, CA: Hay House, Inc.

[40] Perry, B. D., & Szalavitz, M. (2017). *The boy who was raised as a dog: And other stories from a child psychiatrist's notebook: What traumatized children can teach us about loss, love, and healing.* New York, NY: Basic Books.

Made in the USA
Coppell, TX
07 March 2022